Praise for
Global Franchising Operations Management

"While much has been published in franchising over the years, this book, for perhaps the first time, recognizes the important role franchising is playing in developing countries and emerging markets around the world. As a franchise consultant for close to 30 years, I found the case studies to be as fascinating as they were informative."

—Mark C. Siebert, CEO, The iFranchise Group, Inc., www.ifranchisegroup.com, USA

"Ilan Alon, a superb researcher and scholar on international business and franchising, continues to add significantly to the field in his new publication, *Global Franchising Operations Management*. A prolific writer with experience in Asia, Europe, and the Middle East, Ilan has published more than 100 articles in prestigious and diverse international journals in addition to authoring many noteworthy books."

—Cheryl R. Babcock, CFE, Director, International Institute for Franchise Education (IIFE), H. Wayne Huizenga School of Business & Entrepreneurship; Executive Director, International Society of Franchising (ISoF), USA

"Franchising is booming everywhere—in most countries of the world (developed and emerging markets) and most industries (retailing and services). The cases presented in this book cover many countries, many industries, and many topics of interest for the franchising practitioners. The relevant analysis of these cases by Dr. Ilan Alon gives an overview of the various issues (marketing, management, logistics…) faced by franchisors when internationalizing their network. This book contributes to the better understanding of practitioners (franchisors, franchisees…) and also students regarding franchising globally."

—Dr. Rozenn Perrigot, Associate Professor and Head of the MSc in Franchising at the Graduate School of Management at the University of Rennes 1 in France, Researcher at the Center for Research in Economics and Management (CREM UMR CNRS 6211), and Consultant in Franchising

"This is an important contribution to the field of international franchising knowledge and education. The case studies presented illuminate a wide gambit of issues facing prospective and existing franchisors and franchisees alike. Coupled with the wide range of business types, stages of development, countries and contexts discussed, the issues raised expose the reader to many crucial and contemporary franchising questions. At the same time, the reader comes away with some very interesting insights into the franchising programs of some well-known companies, like Marks and Spencer, Kodak Express, and The Athlete's Foot."

—Callum Floyd, Director, Franchize Consultants, New Zealand

"Dr. Ilan Alon is the authority in relation to international franchising and emerging markets. His depth of knowledge and practical advice, guidance, and insight are invaluable. *Global Franchising Operations Management* is an essential resource for any franchise professional engaged in international development."

—**Paul Cairnie**, CEO, World Franchise Associates, Ukraine

"Franchise professionals will appreciate the inside information…it's not only educational, it's also entertaining (which makes me wish I had been one of the contributors)."

—**Dr. John P. Hayes**, Gulf University for Science & Technology, Kuwait, Webmaster: www.FranchiseMastermind.com; www.HowtoBuyaFranchise.com

"This book is really interesting, especially for aspiring entrepreneurs and franchise professionals. Ilan Alon seeks to provide a framework for franchisors who wish to expand their brand locally as well as internationally. I highly recommend this book."

—**Dhawal Shah**, Founder, Way2Franchise, India

"Groundbreaking, critical information on franchising. A must-read!"

—**Dianne H.B. Welsh**, Ph.D., Hayes Distinguished Professor of Entrepreneurship, Director of Cross-Disciplinary Programs, The University of North Carolina Greensboro, USA

Global Franchising
Operations Management

Global Franchising Operations Management

Cases in International and Emerging Markets Operations

Ilan Alon

Vice President, Publisher: Tim Moore
Associate Publisher and Director of Marketing: Amy Neidlinger
Executive Editor: Jeanne Glasser
Editorial Assistant: Pamela Boland
Operations Specialist: Jodi Kemper
Senior Marketing Manager: Julie Phifer
Assistant Marketing Manager: Megan Graue
Cover Designer: Chuti Prasertsith
Managing Editor: Kristy Hart
Senior Project Editor: Lori Lyons
Copy Editor: Karen Annett
Proofreader: Katherine Ruiz
Indexer: Erika Millen
Senior Compositor: Gloria Schurick
Manufacturing Buyer: Dan Uhrig

Pearson Education, Inc.
Publishing as FT Press
Upper Saddle River, New Jersey 07458

IVEY Reprinted with the permission of the Richard Ivey School of Business Foundation and
Ivey Publishing.

This book is sold with the understanding that neither the author nor the publisher is engaged
in rendering legal, accounting, or other professional services or advice by publishing this
book. Each individual situation is unique. Thus, if legal or financial advice or other expert
assistance is required in a specific situation, the services of a competent professional should
be sought to ensure that the situation has been evaluated carefully and appropriately. The
author and the publisher disclaim any liability, loss, or risk resulting directly or indirectly,
from the use or application of any of the contents of this book.

FT Press offers excellent discounts on this book when ordered in quantity for bulk purchases or special
sales. For more information, please contact U.S. Corporate and Government Sales, 1-800-382-3419,
corpsales@pearsontechgroup.com. For sales outside the U.S., please contact International Sales at
international@pearson.com.

Company and product names mentioned herein are the trademarks or registered trademarks of their
respective owners.

First Printing March 2012

ISBN-10: 0-13-288414-3
ISBN-13: 978-0-13-288414-3

Pearson Education LTD.
Pearson Education Australia PTY, Limited.
Pearson Education Singapore, Pte. Ltd.
Pearson Education Asia, Ltd.
Pearson Education Canada, Ltd.
Pearson Educatión de Mexico, S.A. de C.V.
Pearson Education—Japan
Pearson Education Malaysia, Pte. Ltd.

Library of Congress Cataloging-in-Publication Data

Alon, Ilan.

 Global franchising operations management : cases in international and emerging markets operations /
Ilan Alon.

  p. cm.

 ISBN 978-0-13-288414-3 (hardback : alk. paper)

 1. Franchises (Retail trade) 2. International trade. 3. Franchises (Retail trade)--Case studies. I. Title.

 HF5429.23.A376 2012

 658.8'708--dc23

2011041875

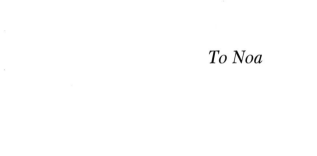

To Noa

Table of Contents

Acknowledgments

This book is a compilation of multiple years of research work and field studies with multiple individuals. I would like to thank my case coauthors who contributed to the development of the individualized cases:

Aleksandar Erceg (Croatia)

Allen H. Kupetz (United States)

Amber Xu (China)

David M. Currie (United States)

Eve Misati (United States)

Mirla Alpeza (Croatia)

The three U.S.-based authors are my colleagues from Rollins College, *U.S. News and World Report* #1 University and College among the Southeast Regional Universities.

I would also like to thank FT Press/Pearson Education Consulting Editor and Harwood Professor of Operations Management Emeritus, Rollins College, Barry Render, Ph.D., for his years of friendship and mentorship; and FT Press Executive Editor Jeanne Glasser for her guidance and support.

About the Author

Ilan Alon, Ph.D., is Cornell Professor of International Business at Rollins College and visiting scholar at Harvard Kennedy School.

Dr. Alon has developed and taught franchising courses in China (Fudan University and China Europe International Business School, CEIBS), Italy (MIB School of Management), Germany (Jacobs University), and India (Integrated Institute for Learning and Management, IILM). He has lectured extensively on franchising in various professional associations, including the International Franchise Association, International Society for Franchising, and the Academy of International Business.

Dr. Alon consulted USAID on franchising development in emerging markets. In Croatia, he aided in the development of the field of franchising through education to bankers, business consultants, and lawyers and provided support for budding home-grown franchisors. He has also consulted multinational companies, such as Duhan (Croatia) and illy (Italy), to develop their franchising systems.

A prolific author on Global Franchising, Dr. Alon's books include:

Franchising Globally: Innovation, Learning and Imitation (Palgrave, 2010)

Service Franchising: A Global Perspective (Springer, 2005)

International Franchising in Industrialized Markets: Western and Northern Europe (CCH Inc., 2003)

International Franchising in Industrialized Markets: North America, Pacific Rim and Other Developed Countries (CCH Inc., 2002)

International Franchising in Emerging Markets: China, India, and Other Asian Countries (CCH Inc., 2001)

International Franchising in Emerging Markets: Central and Eastern Europe and Latin America (CCH Inc., 2001)

The Internationalization of US Franchising Systems (Garland Publishing, 1999)

1

Introduction

What is a franchise? According to the International Franchise Association, the industry's lobby group, "A franchise is the agreement or license between two legally independent parties which gives:

- A person or group of people (franchisee) the right to market a product or service using the trademark or trade name of another business (franchisor)
- The franchisee the right to market a product or service using the operating methods of the franchisor
- The franchisee the obligation to pay the franchisor fees for these rights
- The franchisor the obligation to provide rights and support to franchisees[1]

Franchising is a commercial relationship between two entities in which one of the entities, the franchisor, grants the other entity, the franchisee, the right to use its commercial and intellectual assets for a period of time in return for fees and royalties. Fees are often expressed as a fixed sum paid in advance, and royalties are often expressed as a percentage of gross revenues. The nature of the relationship between the franchisor and the franchisee is determined by the institutions that govern franchising—franchise law, as well as the personal and commercial relations developed between the franchisee and the franchisor. Because franchising is often defined by the legal environment, multiple variations exist. Italian franchising law promulgated in April of 2004, for example, defines franchising as "a contract by which one party grants to the other, for a consideration, the use of combination of intellectual property and/or industrial rights, know-how, technical and commercial assistance, as well as the opportunity to be part of a franchising network." Governance by contract means that appropriate institutions to enforce and support franchising should exist. The contract defines the roles and obligations of the parties.

Franchising is a hybrid form of business. It requires the franchisee to follow the rules of operations, or the franchisee may lose his/her rights to the franchise. In this way, franchising is less entrepreneurial than the stand-alone business. However, the franchisee is often an owner-operator who has a significant investment, both in time and money, built into the system. The franchisee's engagement with the business—taking risks, solving problems, and operating the business—qualifies him/her as an entrepreneur. Because the franchisee has no boss in the traditional sense, he/she is really not an employee. Therefore, the franchisee is somewhere between being an employee (whose actions are monitored and controlled) to an entrepreneur (whose actions lead to residual income). In this way, franchising possesses both marketlike relations and firmlike relations. The extent to which franchisees can act entrepreneurially depends on the size of the franchisor, how franchising is embedded within the franchisor, the legal relationship, the operational autonomy, the commercial interdependence, and the extent of mutual benefits.

From an operations perspective, franchising is a systematized method of transferring organizational know-how to agents (franchisees) while minimizing the risks involved in making investments. To the marketers, franchising is a way to reach optimal distribution, perhaps in areas where the company's own tentacles cannot overreach. Franchising can also be viewed as a financial vehicle for both passive and active investors. Real estate developers might want to buy the rights to develop certain retail concepts when building a regional mall, for example. Such developers often buy multiple units at a time and multiple concepts to fit their desired developmental plans. Master international franchising has become the most popular method for expanding overseas as it allows one entity the control and responsibility for the development of entire countries or regions within countries. In short, franchising is a contractual agreement, a hybrid form of business, a method of distribution, a mode of entry into a new country, a financial investment, and a method of operations.

There are various advantages and disadvantages to the franchisor and the franchisee. The franchisee's biggest benefit is the slogan used by the industry: "be in business for yourself but not by yourself." The franchisee can benefit from the franchisors' brand-name recognition, proven products and methods, proven marketing systems, proven technology, know-how and competitiveness in the industry, financial assistance from the franchisor or a banking affiliate, pooled resources, and economies of scale in advertising and buying. However, the franchise dream is sometime unfulfilled as the franchisee finds that results are based on hard work and resource commitment is insufficient. Fees and royalties have to be paid, contractually, even if the residual income of the franchisee is nonexistent. The franchisor has much power over the franchisee's operations, contract, and, therefore, in legal disputes.

In addition, many benefits accrue to the franchisor. Franchisors who reach a critical level of output can spread the fixed costs over a greater number of outlets, giving them a competitive cost structure. Increased purchasing power against suppliers, economies of scale, additional capital, and the potential to expand the brand quickly are some of the benefits of franchising. On the other hand, franchisors are sometimes troubled by monitoring the franchisees' actions, controlling quality, protecting their brand, getting into legal disputes, sharing revenues with franchisees, creating new future competitors, and limiting operational flexibility. Conflict with franchisees can lead to dissolution for a small franchisor. Failure to control for quality can lead to the deterioration of the total brand and to eventual closure.

Like a marriage, the focus of successful franchising relies on the ability of the partners to work together harmoniously. This means that franchisees are empowered and engaged, that there is a mutual commitment from both sides, and that relational norms embody flexibility and trust. Cooperative relations emerge from good franchisee selection and training, shared decision making, adherence to ethical standards, and, perhaps most important, profitable businesses.

Franchising is a huge part of the modern global economy. In the U.S. economy alone, it represents about 785 million establishments with an output that approaches $740 billion (see Table 1.1). International markets for franchising are also growing. In the United States, franchising accounts for nearly 18 million jobs (1 of 8) and a $2.1 trillion contribution to output[2] (see Table 1.2). Although reliable statistics are not available, several books have documented international growth in recent years through a variety of country and industry studies.[3] See Table 1.3 for franchise associations around the world.

Table 1.1 Franchising in the United States

Business Lines	Establishments	Employment (Thousands)	Output (Billions of Dollars)		(Billions of Dollars)	
	Amount	Percent Change Over Prior Year	Amount	Percent Change Over Prior Year	Amount	Percent Change Over Prior Year
Automotive	31,659	3.9%	$185	3.9%	$39.7	7.2%
Business services	92,714	-0.2%	$819	-0.2%	$128.7	3.5%
Commercial and residential services	70,129	3.7%	$281	3.7%	$45.8	6.9%
Lodging	26,011	4.4%	$711	4.4%	$70.8	4.0%
Personal services	130,895	2.5%	$602	2.5%	$86.2	6.5%
Quick service restaurants	152,665	2.6%	$2,982	2.6%	$194.0	4.9%
Real estate	86,825	1.1%	$341	1.1%	$51.2	0.1%
Retail food	60,841	3.2%	$484	3.2%	$38.2	6.2%
Retail products and services	99,592	3.9%	$402	3.9%	$29.5	5.7%
Table/full service restaurants	33,471	2.3%	$1,003	2.3%	$55.7	4.6%
Total	**784,802**	**2.5%**	**$7,808**	**2.5%**	**$739.9**	**4.7%**

Table 1.2 U.S. Jobs and Output from Franchising

	Percent of U.S. Nonfarm Private Sector	Because of Franchised Businesses
Jobs	11.8%	17,430,700
Payroll	9.7%	$707.6 billion
Output	9.0%	$2.1 trillion
GDP	9.7%	$1.2 trillion

This book is divided into three parts:

Part I: To Franchise or Not to Franchise

Part II: In Search of Global Opportunities

Part III: Franchising in Emerging Markets and Developing Countries

Multiple franchising systems from different industries (coffee, supermarket, clothing, photography, food, athletic wear, and farming) and different countries (Croatia, Korea, United Kingdom, United States, China, and Indonesia) are represented. The diversity of companies/industries and countries in this book gives a panoramic overview of franchising around the world, across both time and space. Executives who read this book will learn about franchising success and failures through case studies. Students of franchising will learn the key success factors of franchising around the world, best practices, and will be given the opportunity to identify franchising problems and solutions. The last chapter of the book provides insight into each of the cases along with the epilogue based on what happened after the case was written.

The first part of the book discusses the decision to franchise and offers chapters with cases on coffee franchising in Croatia and Korea, as well as an example of a large UK retailer. The first two cases, featured in Chapters 2, "San Francisco Coffee House: An American-Style Franchise in Croatia," and 3, "Trying to Create a Stir: Opening a Coffee Shop in Korea," examine the decision to franchise from both the franchisor point of view and the franchisee point of view. In Chapter 2, the franchisor has developed a franchise system, but the system is new and the environment is not auspicious to franchising due to its immaturity and lack of supporting institutions. In the case, Tensek and Pacek are faced with the problem of should they franchise or not and, if so, how should they go about doing so. Chapter 3 supplements Chapter 2's case very well because it focuses on the franchisee perspective, looking at the same industry. There, two would-be entrepreneurs, Min-Guk "MG" Kim and Kevin Andes, attempt to evaluate whether to buy a coffee franchise in Korea. Both domestic and foreign options existed, as well as the option to open their own storefront. Chapter 4, "International Marketing and Franchising at Marks & Spencer," is differentiated from Chapters 2 and 3 as it shows how franchising is implemented in a large corporate setting. M&S is the largest UK retailer and franchising is only used in the international marketplace, in places that the company does not want to invest because of a limited market and/or high exposure to risk. Franchising has a trade-off between risk and return. While the financial risks are relatively low, the potential return is limited to the royalty stream.

Part II of the book specifically deals with the international environment, first by measuring potential demand in Chapter 5, "Estimating Demand in Emerging Markets for Kodak Express," for Kodak Express, and then selecting an international market for a steak concept from the United States in Chapter 6, "Ruth's Chris Steak House: The High Stakes of International Expansion." Market assessment and selection are interrelated aspects of successful internationalization. Estimating the potential demand is one of the prerequisites for targeting a country for international expansion. The case in Chapter 5 shows how companies can use country-level statistics to estimate the potential demand. Using income distribution and family size, the case shows how to calculate the economic potential starting with GDP. Making some assumptions about income elasticity of demand, the manager can estimate the market potential for a concept. Chapter 6 presents the analyst with the problem of how to target a country using a restaurant concept as a case. Using statistics on beef consumption and income per capita, the analyst is asked to choose the most appropriate markets for expansion, where the manager is expected to make an investment.

The third and final part of the book focuses on franchising in emerging markets and developing countries. Multiunit franchising arrangements are popular among emerging markets and developing countries. In these markets, a franchisee may be a company or a rich individual or family business that is able to purchase and develop the region. The company is often connected to the local culture and customs and is able to make the adaptations needed as well as monitor and control the system expansion. In a sense, the master franchisee becomes the subfranchisor in a given location. The master franchisee collects the fees, shares the royalties with the franchisor, and is responsible to the administration and management of the system in the host market. Chapters 7, "Master International Franchising in China: The Athlete's Foot, Inc. (Part A)," and 8, "Master International Franchising in China: The Athlete's Foot, Inc. (Part B)," feature the case of a master franchisee Rick Wang, owner of RetailCo, who franchised the American Athlete's Foot concept in China. At the time of entry, the situation was ideal, large pent-up demand for branded athletic shoes was matched by opening for space in department stores and on street fronts. Shortly after opening and expanding the Athlete's Foot system in China, Rick got into trouble and started to lose sales to the brands themselves that opened direct channels to the consumers. How Rick has managed to avoid financial collapse is instructive to would-be master franchisees considering a purchase of a foreign system into an emerging market. The last case, presented in Chapter 9, "Social Entrepreneurship and Sustainable Farming in Indonesia," shows how franchising can be used to create social change. In this organic farming case situated in Indonesia, microfranchising is proposed as a model to expand this social business. Microfranchising is franchising for the bottom of the pyramid and these businesses attempt to be inclusive to the poorest.

Collectively, the cases presented in these chapters show managers how to think about franchising from a multinational and multi-industry perspective. Both franchisee and franchisor considerations and problems are discussed. The final chapter shows what has actually transpired and provides an analysis and epilogue, where available, for each of the cases. It is hoped that this book, along with the cases presented, will show future practitioners how to franchise, under different institutional environments, and how to select and operate in different world markets.

Table 1.3 National Franchise Associations, Members of World Franchise Council, WFC

ARGENTINA—Argentinean Franchise Association (AAF)
Lucas Secades, Executive Director
www.aafranchising.com
info@aafranchising.com.ar

AUSTRALIA—Franchise Council of Australia (FCA)
George Yammouni, Chairman
Steve Wright, President and CEO
www.franchise.org.au
info@franchise.org.au

AUSTRIA—Austrian Franchise Association
Andreas Schwerla, Chairman
Susanne Seifert, Managing Director
susanne.seifert@franchise.at
www.franchise.at
oefv@franchise.at

BELGIUM—Belgian Franchise Federation (BFF)
Didier Depreay, Chairman
dd@fbf-bff.be
Gilbert Lardinois, Secretary General
www.fbf-bff.be

BRAZIL—Brazilian Franchise Association (ABF)
Ricardo Bomeny, Chairman
Ricardo Camargo, Executive Director
www.abf.com.br
abf@abf.com.br

CANADA—Canadian Franchise Association (CFA)
Lorraine McLachlan, President and CEO
www.cfa.ca
info@cfa.ca

CHINA—Chain-Store & Franchise Association (CCFA)
Guo Geping, President
Lucy Wu Rui Ling, Vice Secretary General
lucywu@ccfa.org.cn
www.ccfa.org.cn

CROATIA—Croatian Franchise Association (CAF/FIP)
Ljiljana Kukecs, Chairman
www.fip.com.hr
udruga@fip.com/hr

CZECH REPUBLIC—Czech Franchise Association (CAF)
Ivo Lamich, Chairman
Hana Juraskova, Managing Director
www.czech-franchise.cz
caf@czech-franchise.cz

DENMARK—Danish Franchise Association (DFA)
Inger Fredsted, Chairman
Toke Allentoft, Managing Director
ta@dk-franchise.dk
www.dk-franchise.dk

ECUADOR—Ecuadorian Franchise Association (AEFRAN)
Ing. Guido Santillán, Executive Director
www.aefran.org/index/html
expo@aefran.org

EGYPT—Egyptian Franchise Development Association (EFDA)
Moataz Al Alfi, Chairman
Hussein Abou El Fath, Secretary General
www.efda.org.eg
info@efda.org.eg

EUROPEAN UNION—European Franchise Federation (EFF)
Dieter Frohlich, Chairman
Carol Chopra, Executive Director
www.eff-franchise.com
info@eff-franchise.com

FINLAND—Finnish Franchising Association (FFF)
Veli Pekka Pihlainen, Chairman
Juha Vastamäki, Managing Director
www.franchising.fi
office@franchising.fi

FRANCE—French Franchise Federation (FFF)
Guy Gras, Chairman
Chantal Zimmer, General Director
c.zimmer@franchise-fff.com
www.franchise-fff.com

GERMANY—German Franchise Association (DFV)
Dieter Frohlich, Chairman
Torben L. Brodersen, Managing Director
brodersen@franchiseverband.com
www.franchiseverband.com

GREAT BRITAIN—British Franchise Association (BFA)
Mike Goddard, Chairman
Brian Smart, General Director
b.smart@thebfa.org
www.thebfa.org
mailroom@thebfa.org

GREECE—Greek Franchise Association
I. Illiadis, Chairman
S. Yanakakis, General Director
www.franchising.gr
franchiseassociation@franchising.gr

HONG KONG—Hong Kong Franchise Association (HKFA)
Charlotte Chow, General Manager
www.franchise.org.hk
hkfa@franchise.org.hk

HUNGARY—Hungarian Franchise Association (HFA)
Laszlo Muranyi, Chairman
Katalin Mandel, Managing Director
www.franchise.hu
info@franchise.hu

INDIA—Franchise Association of India (FAI)
C. Yoginder Pal, Chairman
Dhruv Jaywant, CEO
dhruv@jaywant@fai.co.in
www.fai.co.in

ITALY—Italian Franchise Association (AIF)
G. Fiorelli, Chairman
Italo Bussoli, Managing Director
www.assofranchising.it
assofranchising@assofranchising.it

JAPAN—Japanese Franchise Association (JFA)
Kiyoshi Hijikata, Chairman
Tomoyuki Kimura, Managing Director
tkimura@jfa-fc.or.jp
www.jfa-fc.or.jp

KAZAKHSTAN—Kazakhstan Franchise Association
Andrey Zakharov
kazaf@mail.ru
Web site not available

KOREA—Korean Franchise Association (KFA)
Kim Yung Man, Chairman
Park Kee Young, Vice Chairman
kypark@gymboree.co.kr
www.ikfa.or.kr

LEBANON—Lebanese Franchise Association (LFA)
Charles Arbid, Chairman
www.lfalebanon.com
president@lfalebanon.com

MALAYSIA—Malaysian Franchise Association (MFA)
Abdul Malik Abdullah, Chairman
Ahmad Faizal Mohamed Noor, General Manager
www.mfa.org.my
wfc.affairs@mfa.org.my

MEXICO—Mexican Franchise Association (MFA)
Diego Elizarraras, Chairman
www.franquiciasdemexico.org
Presidencia@franquiciasdemexico.org

MORROCO—Moroccan Franchise Association (FMF)
Miss Btissam Omari
www.fmf.ma
omari@fmf.ma

NETHERLANDS—Netherlands Franchise Association
Maarten Dorhout Mees, Chairman
Jos Burgers, Executive Director
www.nfv.nl
info@nfv.nl

NEW ZEALAND—Franchise Association of New Zealand (FANZ)
Estelle Logan, Chairman
Graham Billings, Executive Director
graham@franchise.org.nz
www.franchiseassociation.org.nz

PHILIPPINES—Phillipines Franchise Association (PFA)
Robert F. Trota, Chairman
Chit Estrada, Executive Director
www.pfa.org.ph
international@pfa.org.ph

PORTUGAL—Portuguese Franchise Association (APF)
P. Antunes, Chairman
www.apfranchise.org
geral@apf.org.pt

RUSSIA—Russian Franchise Association (RARF)
Merab Elashvili, Chairman
Yury Mikhaylichenko, Managing Director
www.rarf.ru
rusfranch@yandex.ru

SINGAPORE—Franchising and Licensing Association (FLA)
C. Chandroo, Chairman
Terry Wong, General Manager
terry@flasingapore.org
www.flasingapore.org

SLOVENIA—Slovenian Franchise Association (SFA)
Milan Stegne, Chairman
Igor Pavlin, Secretary
igor.pavlin@guest.arnes.si
www.franchise-slovenia.net

SOUTH AFRICA—Franchise Association of South Africa (FASA)
Kobus Oosthuizen, Chairman
Vera Valasis, Managing Director
vera.valasis@fasa.co.za
www.fasa.co.za

SWEDEN—Swedish Franchise Association (SFF)
Jonas Idestrom, Chairman
Anders Svensson, Managing Director
anders@franchiseforeningen.se
www.franchiseforeningen.se

SWITZERLAND—Swiss Franchise Association (SFV)
Cristoph Wildhaber, CEO
www.franchiseverband.ch
franchise-fr@franchiseverband.ch

TAIWAN—Taiwan Franchise Association (TCFA)
Chung-Jen Hsu, Chairman
www.tcfa.org.tw
tcfa@tcfa.org.tw

TURKEY—Turkish Franchise Association (UFRAD)
Mustafa Aydin, Chairman
Gurkan Donat, Vice Chairman
www.ufrad.org.tr
ufrad@ufrad.com.tr

Endnotes

1. http://franchise.org/franchiseesecondary.aspx?id=52625 (accessed July 8, 2011)

2. http://www.buildingopportunity.com/download/National%20 Views.pdf (accessed July 8, 2011)

3. See, for example, Alon, Ilan. *Franchising Globally*. New York: Palgrave MacMillan, 2010. Alon, Ilan. *Service Franchising: A Global Perspective*. New York: Springer, 2005.

Part I

To Franchise or Not to Franchise

2

San Francisco Coffee House:
An American-Style Franchise in Croatia

Ilan Alon, Mirela Alpeza, Aleksandar Erceg

On the return to their homeland of Croatia following a six-year visit to the United States, Denis Tensek and Jasmina Pacek decided to open an American-style coffee house reminiscent of San Francisco's atmosphere. Although Croatia had many coffee houses, few had the combination of service, quality, products, and atmosphere that they remembered from their time living in the United States.

Tensek and Pacek started with a single coffee house. From the beginning, they felt that it had the potential to grow into a franchise. Instead of purchasing a franchise from someone else, they considered creating one that had all the elements of the modern franchise chains that were available on the international market plus the adjustments needed to the local market. They decided to use all of their U.S. lifestyle and professional experiences as well as their understanding of habits and behaviors of the local maront to create this new local concept in Croatia.

The initial coffee house became a success. The business steadily grew and operating profits had reached a satisfactory level. Motivated with the success of the first coffee shop in one of Croatia's poorest regions, the couple realized that the potential for this concept was national, if not regional. But, how would they grow? Should they develop their own outlets or open more company-owned outlets?

Growing organically by opening self-owned stores was costly, slow, and hard to control. They had neither the means nor the staff.

They knew they did not want to put more capital at risk, and did not have the time to travel to various locations around the country. Furthermore, their concept had started to garner local publicity, and inquiries from would-be franchisees began to arise. But, how could they franchise in Croatia?

Croatia had a small economy, a changing legal system, and little experience in franchising. Growing through franchising was appealing, but they only had one store, the business was young, and franchising was unfamiliar to the emerging market of Croatia. The conditions for franchising were not ideal.

Aside from whether to franchise or not, how could they protect their intellectual property and business format know-how? How could they fight off imitators? What would happen if Starbucks or other major coffee chains entered the market? What should be the next steps? How could they become the biggest and most successful coffee house nationally or regionally?

The Entrepreneurs: Tensek and Pacek

Tensek had an MBA from California State University and extensive experience working in large U.S. corporations. Pacek, on the other hand, had a master's degree in fine arts and design from the University of California, and had worked as an art director in several U.S. companies. The couple's successful careers and profitable real estate investments in the United States gave them the comfort, confidence, and capital to return to Croatia to invest in a new venture while helping their country's development at the same time. They wanted to create a business in Croatia that was world class, towering above local offerings in service, quality, and satisfying customer expectations.

Tensek and Pacek recalled their days in the United States and the economic success stories of all the major coffee franchise chains such as Starbucks. They even considered taking a master franchise license for Croatia, but the process was long, complicated, and extremely expensive in comparison with the expected return. The fact was that Starbucks had very low local brand recognition in Croatia. The other problem with imported brands was that they often did not allow the adjustments needed to succeed in local markets—the major one being the pricing of their product when it was simply too high for the local purchasing power of a developing country such as Croatia. They therefore decided to open the San Francisco Coffee House (SFCH) in 2003, a coffee shop with a recognizable visual identity—an interior in which visitors could feel the San Francisco-style coffee shop atmosphere.

The Opening of "San Francisco Coffee House"

Osijek was a town with many coffee shops and bars, and visiting them was part of the lifestyle of the local population. But there was one competitive problem from which they all suffered: They all offered roughly the same limited product line without any differentiating concept. Tensek and Pacek noticed that what was missing in the market was an American-style coffee bar, in which most of the offerings would consist of different types of coffee, and that would include the novel (in Croatia) possibility of getting "coffee to go." They decided to adapt this ubiquitous American concept to the local Croatian market. They were under the impression that the "Made in USA" brand would be positively received in their "new" market, so they named the coffee bar the "San Francisco Coffee House." During the development of the business plan, Tensek traveled several times to the United States researching ideas, studying the technology of coffee making, and personally bringing back with him some of the supplies and crucial ingredients.

Tensek had chosen the location for the San Francisco Coffee House carefully: He was looking for a location with a minimum of 80 square meters near an area with heavy foot traffic because his and Pacek's main target market was to be businesspeople. He found an excellent location in the town's center—across from the green market, near three university departments, and several lawyers' and public notaries' offices—for which he signed a five-year lease with provisions for extending the lease and a right to preemptive purchase in case the owner wanted to sell the premise. After the first few months, they found that their major client markets were students and business professionals of all ages.

Because SFCH was the first American coffee house in Croatia, this unique place where one could enjoy the authentic ambience of the American city received excellent reviews and unusually large media attention in the first six months of existence. *Elle Décor* ranked it among six best-decorated service industry interiors in the country, complimenting the brave mixture of styles and materials Pacek used to create the urban, bright, and sophisticated environment. This was particularly commendable given the entrepreneurs' limited start-up capital of €40,000.

The San Francisco Coffee House assortment was also unique for this market. It offered its customers coffee in 17 different latte (with milk) and mocha variants and American-style muffins in several varieties. Coffee could be taken in the relaxing but urban atmosphere of the bar or it could be taken out in "to-go" packaging. However, SFCH did not have its own coffee brand; instead, in the SFCH in Osijek, coffee cups were marked with a coffee supplier's logo. Coffee suppliers in Croatia also customarily provided the coffee-making machines and their service free of charge (or the cost was included in the price of every kilogram of coffee). In order for Tensek and Pacek to adapt to their target market, guests were provided Croatian and international newspapers and magazines and free wireless access to the Internet (which was extremely rare in Croatia). The ambience was also enhanced by smooth jazz and billboard music from the 1970s, 1980s, and 1990s.

SFCH had eight employees and was managed by Tanja Ivelj. The employees were all young people, some of them without any previous working experience and most of whom had worked in SFCH from its inception. When searching for employees, Tensek looked for trustworthy, loyal, and honest people. For each workstation, employees had a detailed job description and detailed checklists for each shift and for weekly and monthly routine duties.

All employees underwent training for working in a coffee shop/ bar. Their salaries were almost 20 percent higher than those of comparable employees at other local coffee shops. Every six months, all employees had scheduled performance reviews. If a review was satisfactory, there was a further 5 percent salary increase. Human resource management was one of the areas where Tensek had brought his American corporate experience into Croatia. In Croatia, employee rights, salaries, and general terms of employment were, in most cases, ambiguous. Also contrary to the common practice in Croatia, SFCH provided full paid vacation and benefits for its employees. As a result, in an industry where the turnover rate was extremely high, the San Francisco Coffee House was able to achieve less than 20 percent turnover over the first three years of operation. As Tensek mentioned, "Satisfied and motivated employees offer a high standard of service to the end customers."

SFCH made an extra effort to maintain excellent relationships with its suppliers, making timely payments in a market that was known for its irregularities. Wise and responsible financial management was the company's priority. The summary of the financial performance of the company's operations is shown in Table 2.1.

Table 2.1 SFCH Financial Performance

Income Data	2006 (Euros)	2007 (Euros)
Net revenues	133,332	166,666
Direct costs	50,666	54,000
Gross profit	82,666	112,666
Operating expenses	36,000	39,333
EBITDA	46,666	73,333
Taxes	9,680	14,520
Depreciation	2,666	7,333

The Environment for Franchising in Croatia

The environment for franchising in Croatia was not ideal because of insufficient regulation, little market know-how about franchising, and low economic development. On the other hand, the emerging market and the new openness to European integration had created opportunities to start bringing in new businesses from the outside.

The Economic Environment

In 1991, after the Republic of Croatia gained its independence, the Croatian market increasingly opened to a great variety of international products and services. Due to the economic growth, which began in the late 1990s, salaries had grown appreciably, especially in the larger cities and in certain other parts of Croatia.[1] Basic statistics on the economy are shown in Table 2.2.

Table 2.2 Basic Socioeconomic Data on Croatia

Annual Data	2007	Historical Averages (percent)	2003–2007
Population (m)	4.0	Population growth	0.0
GDP (US$ bn; market exchange rate)	51,452	Real GDP growth	4.9
GDP (US$ bn; purchasing power parity)	69,211	Real domestic demand growth	5.0
GDP per head (US$; market exchange rate)	12,863	Inflation	2.6
GDP per head (US$; purchasing power parity)	17,303	Current-account balance (percent of GDP)	–7.1
Exchange rate (av) HRK:US$	5.35(b)	FDI inflows (percent of GDP)	6.4

Source: *The Economist*, 2008, http://www.economist.com/countries/Croatia/profile. cfm?folder=Profile-FactSheet, accessed June 11, 2008.

Salary growth resulted in increased consumer demand for higher-quality world brand names, which were not widely available in Croatia at the time. After independence, the Croatian market became flooded with imported goods of variable quality. The habits of younger Croatian consumers had changed as a result of this increased supply: International brands became the acquisition target of younger consumers, whereas older people tended to continue to seek out domestic brands. Inevitably, perhaps, purchasing habits also varied geographically.[2]

Financial institutions in Croatia were mostly owned by foreign banks—around 90 percent according to one source[3]—and many of these acquisitions had occurred in recent years. Although there was a predictable variety of capitalization options for would-be entrepreneurs, a main characteristic of the Croatian domestic market was the bankruptcy of small entrepreneurs as they struggled to collect their own debts. Although bartering was a common fixture of the domestic market (between local companies), the international ownership of local banks made such traditional arrangements problematic.

Political Environment

Creating a vibrant business environment in accordance with the standards of the European Union (EU) and with countries embedded in the local market economy was one of the major goals of the Croatian government's policies. The government's dedication to the reform of the national economy could be seen in its desire to attract foreign investment for the development of Croatia's domestic and international markets.

Foreign investments in Croatia were regulated by the Company Act and other legal norms. A foreign investor in Croatia had a number of organizational options available according to this act: A foreign investor would invest alone or as a joint-venture partner with a Croatian company or private citizen; there were no constraints as to the percentage of foreign ownership that was possible. In addition, in keeping with the government's desire for foreign investment, investors gained access to a number of newly opened markets; entrants could take advantage of a number of incentives, tax benefits, and customs privileges that were only available to foreign investors.

The Institutions of Franchising

In recent years, the Republic of Croatia had approved a number of laws, which resulted in Croatia's acceptance into the World Trade Organization and CEFTA (Central European Free Trade Agreement); these legal changes also allowed Croatia to begin negotiations for acceptance into the EU. Nevertheless, there was no specific legal basis for franchising in Croatia. Franchising was mentioned in Croatian trade law (Narodne Novine, 2003), where the generalities of potential franchising agreements were stated, but mention was made in only one article and that mention was very condensed. Therefore, there was no legal standard for the development of franchising and no legal parameters (yet) for franchising agreements: Business practices on the ground determined the appropriateness of such agreements.

Because the concept of franchising was relatively new to Croatia and to its inhabitants, little knowledge existed about franchising. There were two Centers for Franchising, one in Osijek and one in Zagreb, Croatia's most vibrant city. Each of these centers had worked with the Croatian Franchising Association to stimulate franchising development in several ways:

- **Educating about franchising**—The Franchise Center in Osijek, for example, had organized seminars, "Franchise A to Z," in order to educate entrepreneurs about franchising and its benefits.

- **Franchising promotion**—Both centers and the association were trying to promote franchising as a way of doing business through local media: interviews, articles in the newspapers and magazines, and so on.

- **Creating Web sites with information about franchising on the Internet**—The portal contained information such as current news about franchising in Croatia, information about new franchisors, and newly opened franchised locations. It connected franchisors with potential franchisees—one section of the franchise portal contained offers from franchisors interested in the Croatian market; there were several inquiries each week from potential franchisees.

- **Helping domestic companies to become franchisors**—The Franchise Center in Osijek, with the help of Poduzetna Hrvatska, organized training for potential franchise consultants who could help domestic companies if they decided to use franchising as a growth strategy.

- **Establishing franchise fairs and round tables**

Foreign franchises tended to choose one of two potential pathways into the Croatian market: distribution-product franchising and/or business-format franchising. Larger, better-known franchisors like McDonald's opened their offices in Croatia and offered franchises to interested entrepreneurs in order to ensure quality control, while smaller and less well-known franchisors sold master franchises to local entrepreneurs in order to ensure the benefits of local knowledge and cost savings.

Barriers to Franchising Development

During September 2006, The Franchise Center of the Center for Entrepreneurship in Osijek conducted a survey of 50 people, asking what examinees (representatives of banks, entrepreneurs, and lawyers) thought about the barriers facing franchising in Croatia. Their responses included the following:

- **Laws**—There was no legal regulation of franchising in Croatia. The word *franchising* was only mentioned in trade law; the absence of clear legal precedent made it difficult for Croatian lawyers to help their clients, especially during the contracting phase—whether franchisor or franchisee, whether foreign or domestic investor.

- **Franchise professionals**—There was a dearth of professionals related to franchising; there were too few educational efforts and too few franchise consultants who could help potential franchisors in developing their own networks or advise franchisees about selecting one.

- **Problems with banks (not familiar with franchising)**—Banks did not recognize franchising as a relatively safe way of entering into a new business and did not have any specialized loans for the franchising industry; according to a survey conducted by The Franchise Center (2006), some banks' representatives said that they would ask a guarantee for a loan from the franchisor; banks were not willing to educate their employees in order to learn about this way of doing business; and banks seemed unable to distinguish between start-up entrepreneurs creating footholds in new franchise sectors and franchisees who were entering preexisting, proven franchise systems.

- **Small market**—Because there were only about four million inhabitants in Croatia, examinees were doubtful that the largest franchisors would come to Croatia due to logistical problems: The perception was that it was much easier to open a location in London than in Croatia. Large and famous franchisors were looking for bigger areas to capture the population, and they often resisted adapting to local standards and prices; smaller franchisors who would have liked to enter Croatia were not as well known to Croatian entrepreneurs and were, therefore, seldom selected.

- **Franchising was not a well-known way of doing business**—People seldom recognized franchising; many thought it was connected with insurance. This was the biggest barrier according to the survey because people were not willing to enter into something with which they were unfamiliar; further seminars and round tables needed to be organized in order to educate entrepreneurs about franchising and its costs/benefits.

According to the above-mentioned survey, there were some identifiable reasons for the relatively slow development of franchising in the Republic of Croatia: entrepreneurial thinking, lack of franchising education, and a weak national franchising association. First, many entrepreneurs would rather own their own companies and have complete "business freedom" than submit to the restrictions they saw as related to becoming part of a system—from production and distribution to sales and to the "forced" cleaning of the premises. Second, Croatian entrepreneurs were not completely familiar with the benefits that would be gained by being a member of a successful franchising system.

Despite such a pessimistic tone, industry experts also reported that there was an excellent chance for franchising in Croatia, that there was the possibility of high growth in this sector (up to 30 percent), and that Croatia's membership in the EU would provide the necessary boost to franchising development. The survey showed that although franchising was not a familiar way of doing business, experts saw a bright future for franchising in Croatia.

Competition

Franchises had become more well-known in Croatia starting in the early 1990s, after the first McDonald's was opened in Zagreb. "McDonald's expansion into the Croatian market has tended to use two franchising methods: direct franchising and business-facility lease arrangements... Such lease arrangements allow for franchisees to become entry-level franchisees using less capital at the outset."[4]

Other franchisors followed McDonald's lead. For example, one of the relatively new restaurant franchising concepts in the Croatian market was the Hungarian company Fornetti, which managed to spread quickly its mini-bakeries business throughout Croatia by using franchising. They were founded in 1997, and by 2007 had more than 3,000 locations in Central and Eastern Europe.[5] Other international franchises represented in Croatia included Benetton, Subway, Dama Service, and Remax.

According to the Croatian Franchise Association, there were approximately 125 (25 of them domestic) franchise systems present in the Croatian market. These systems operated approximately 900 locations and employed almost 16,000 people.[6] Companies in more than 20 industries had chosen franchising as a growth option, with the sales industry and fast-food sectors accounting for more than 20 percent of the market. Other segments with important shares included the tourist industry, rent-a-car companies, courier services, and the fashion industry.

Tables 2.3 and 2.4 show the most well-known foreign and domestic franchisors in Croatia by industry and number of outlets as of 2007.

Table 2.3 Foreign Franchisors in Croatia

Franchisor	Industry	Number of Outlets
McDonald's	Fast food	16 restaurants
Subway	Fast food	6 restaurants
Fornetti	Bakeries	Over 150 locations
Dama service	Refilling toner cartridges	3 locations
Berlitz	Foreign language school	1 location
Firurella	Weight loss center for women	2 locations
Berghoff	Kitchen equipment	3 locations

Source: "Round table — Franchising in Croatia," address given at EFF/IFA International Symposium, Brussels, October 24-25, 2006.

Table 2.4 Domestic Franchisors in Croatia

Franchisor	Industry	Number of Outlets
Elektromaterijal	Household appliances' distribution	Over 50 stores
X-nation	Fashion clothes	40 stores/corners
Rubelj Grill	Grill	17 restaurants
Skandal	Fashion clothes	15 stores
Body Creator	Weight loss center for women	4 centers
Bio & Bio	Health food	3 shops
Bike Express	Courier service	1 location
San Francisco Coffee House	Coffee bar	1 location

Source: "Round table — Franchising in Croatia," address given at EFF/IFA International Symposium, Brussels, October 24-25, 2006.

Although a few restaurant franchisors had already entered the Croatian market, no well-known international coffee houses had done so. Competition for coffee houses was mostly local, dating back to Croatia's early days. Local competitors offered a roughly homogeneous product—coffee—and most did not bother to create a visual identity, a brand, or a new concept. Price, location, and ambiance distinguished one coffee bar from another. Competitive rivalry from abroad, however, was imminent. The question was not if international coffee houses would come, but when?

Coffee consumption in Croatia was quite high; many Croatians spent time between meals, in the morning, or at night at coffee bars, which often also served beer and other alcoholic products. Although regular bars and other restaurants competed with coffee shops for customers, coffee shops were relatively cheaper, providing a comfortable environment for socializing. Suppliers of coffee were many and included both international and local brands. Coffee, itself, was basically a commodity.

What Should Be Done Next?

Tensek and Pacek looked at the facts: Franchising was one of several possible models for business growth and was widely used in economically developed countries throughout the world. Some of the reasons why companies preferred to develop franchise networks rather than grow organically included lower financial investment, lower risk, faster growth, local market knowledge by the franchisee, and the franchisee's motivation to succeed. They wanted these benefits too.

The barriers which the San Francisco Coffee House faced in franchising in the local market were challenging:

- There was just not enough information about franchising; as a result, entrepreneurial and institutional awareness of franchising was quite low.
- There were no well-established support organizations for the development of franchise networks in Croatia; there were only two Entrepreneurship Centers in Croatia that offered services regarding franchise network development.
- There was no significant support from financial institutions; banks failed to recognize the relatively lower risk of investment in start-up entrepreneurs/franchisees than in independent start-up entrepreneurs.

Moreover, the company was still young and unproven in other locations. The couple could simply enjoy their local success. They could open additional stores by themselves. Or they could try to sell franchises of their concept. See Table 2.5 for the entrepreneurs' estimates of store-level expenses and revenues.

Table 2.5 Expected Revenues and Expenses

	Expenses (Based on One Year)	**Euros (€)**
1.	Salaries with benefits	€10,000
	Manager	€6,000
	Waiter 1	€5,333
	Waiter 2	€5,333
	Waiter 3	€5,333
2.	Rent with utilities	€32,000
3.	Marketing, royalties	€2,666
4.	Cost of direct material (based on €666.66 per day)	€72,000
	Total expenses per year	€138,666
	Total income (based on average of €666.66 per day)	€240,000
	Net income in the first year	€101,333

Could the couple develop franchising in a market where local conditions were less than conducive? Could they gain national prominence? The couple had never run a franchising business and did not have the necessary experience and knowledge. How could they overcome the weaknesses they possessed and the environmental threats? How could they seize the opportunities in the marketplace using their unique experiences, capabilities, and strengths?

This case was supported by The Franchise Center, part of the Center for Entrepreneurship Osijek, and Poduzetna Hrvatska, a USAID project in Croatia.

Endnotes

1. Državni zavod za statistiku, "Statistical information 2006," http://www.dzs.hr/Hrv_Eng/StatInfo/pdf/StatInfo2006.pdf, accessed on October 26, 2006.

2. GfK, "Gradani o markama," Survey conducted by GfK, March 2005,http://www.gfk.r/ress/marke.htm,http://www.gfk.hr/press/marke2.htm, accessed on January 3, 2007.

3. Hrvatska narodna banka, "Standardni prezentacijski format," 2006,   http://www.hnb.hr/publikac/prezent/hbanking-sector.pdf, accessed on October 20, 2006.

4. L. Viducic and G. Brcic in I. Alon and D. Welsh, *International Franchising in Emerging Markets: China, India and Other Asian Countries*, CCH Inc., Chicago, 2001, p.217.

5. Mandel, K. "Franchise in Hungary." Address given at The Franchise Center Osijek seminar "Franšiza od A do Ž," Osijek, Croatia, November 2004.

6. Kukec, L. "Round Table—Franchising in Croatia." Address given at EFF/IFA International Symposium, Brussels, Belgium, October 24–25, 2006.

3

Trying to Create a Stir: Opening a Coffee Shop in Korea

Gyewan Moon, Allen H. Kupetz

In July 2010, Min-Guk "MG" Kim and Kevin Andes were sitting together in a Sleepless in Seattle coffee shop next to the southern border of the beautiful Kyungpook National University (KNU) campus in Daegu, South Korea—about 100 minutes south of Seoul via the high-speed KTX train. Kim and Andes were both teaching business courses at KNU for the summer, but wanted to partner and open a coffee shop in Korea. Kim, a Korean native who earned his Ph.D. in the United States, had tremendous knowledge of business management in Korea. Andes was a retired entrepreneur who loved being in Korea and could possibly provide start-up funding for the company: It seemed like a great pairing.

This coffee shop in Daegu did not have branded coffee mugs for sale or any of the logo merchandise that could be purchased in the major branded coffee shops in Korea. For KRW4,000 (about US$3.50) each, they got a kiwi smoothie, a couple small cookies, unlimited free Internet, comfortable chairs, and some gentle background music that did not drown out their conversation. Ironically, neither had ordered coffee. After a discussion concerning this point, the two agreed that this meant that even noncoffee drinkers could find a reason to enjoy all that this kind of coffee shop had to offer; therefore, they decided that this could be a sustainable business even if they were late entering the crowded market.

Kim told Andes that there was no *f* in Hangul, the almost 600-year-old alphabet used in Korea, so a *p* was used in its place for foreign words; thus, *coffee* was pronounced *copy*, which seemed fitting when looking at all the coffee shop brands with multiple outlets in Korea and the hundreds of single-location establishments. The Starbucks model, which itself was a dominant player in Korea, had been replicated successfully with a dizzying array of choices that appeared to offer only subtle differentiation.

A young woman, almost certainly a student at KNU, put her books down on the table next to Kim and Andes. Kim asked her in Korean why she was in this shop at this time. Apparently noticing Andes, she answered in her best English:

> Unlike the restaurant or cafeteria, the coffee shop doesn't push their customers to leave as soon as possible. In the Korean restaurant, they bring some free, small dessert to their customers who are spending a long time there. It looks like a gift from the restaurant, but it means, "please get out of our restaurant as soon as possible." We think the coffee shop is the place where we can spend all day long without any concern from the clerk.

> It is very rare for me to go to the coffee shop alone. It has become one of the steps for the social gathering: First, the restaurant; second, the coffee shop. It is also rare for me to come to a fancy coffee shop like this. I think customers downtown are very sensitive and conscious of the brand name and reputation of the coffee shop. But students choose according to the price, the cozy atmosphere, and the close distance since we don't have cars. Usually I go to KONA coffee on the north side of campus. The cost is very cheap. A Caffe Americano is only KRW1,500. The coffee shop design is simple, but nice. Whenever I go to the KONA coffee shop, there is always a crowd. But today, I need to study without a crowd.

Kim and Andes thanked her, bought her a *fancy* Caffe Americano, and left her to study. Armed only with data from this sample of one, Kim and Andes knew they had a lot of work to do.

Education and the Korean Economic Miracle

South Korea's economic success is as impressive as it is difficult to explain. The country has no diamonds or gold or other precious metals, no oil or natural gas and no particularly productive farmland. Per capita gross domestic product (GDP) in South Korea was less than US$100 at the end of the Korean War in 1953; however, Korea's GDP was more than US$1.3 trillion in 2010[1]—14th in the world and fourth in Asia behind only Japan, China, and India, all of which have significantly larger populations. In 2010, per capita GDP was more than US$20,000,[2] ranking Korea about 50th globally. It is among the world leaders in broadband Internet access and has a wireless telecommunications infrastructure that is one of the best in the world (and is three to five years ahead of that of the United States). It hosted the 1988 Summer Olympic Games and cohosted the 2002 World Cup. Korean women dominate the Ladies Professional Golf Association (LPGA), and Korean men are striking out hitters in Major League Baseball (MLB). South Korean firms have built many of the tallest skyscrapers in the world, and the country boasts more than 50 companies in the *Forbes 2000*.[3] Among the almost 100 countries that became independent following World War II, none of them can come close to this list of achievements; it is not called the *Korean economic miracle* for nothing.

With this creation of wealth, South Koreans are following the consumer path seen in the habits of other wealthy people around the world: First, they buy their own apartments and appliances; second, they buy cars; third, they start to eat out more, and per capita beef consumption starts to rise—and then they start to spend more money on coffee.

Perhaps because of their positions as professors, Kim and Andes were interested in exploring the possibility of integrating their coffee shop business with one or more of Korea's outstanding universities.

Education, more than any other single factor, was directly attributable to Korea's economic success. Korea's highly competitive education system has a series of entrance exams starting in primary school. This, coupled with the Confucian value for education, means that Korean parents spend a high percentage of their disposable income on educational hardware and software, evening and weekend tutors, and expensive English-language programs. Kim and Andes thought that coupling education and coffee might be the differentiator needed to enter a mature market.

The Korean way of studying is quite different from that of students in the West. Korean students normally spend a lot of time in libraries where they not only study, but they also catch some sleep and meet with friends; they can spend all day—and all night—studying. A European student studying in Korea shared this observation:

> During the exam period, a library is open 24 hours. I was very curious about that. It seemed strange to me so I went there at midnight. I sat there for 3 hours, just observing, to see whether they were in fact working. I was the only westerner there—no European would study this way. But there were a lot of Koreans, even at 3:00 a.m. The library was full. Many students were working on their notebooks or reading something. Those who weren't went outside where they could talk with friends, take a rest, or eat something. I saw them sleeping on desks, covered with blankets. In fact, they seemed to be able to sit there with only short breaks all day and night.[4]

It had become obvious that many Korean students were moving from libraries to comfortable coffee shops to study, take a brief nap, meet with friends, drink coffee, and eat light snacks. There were more than 400 colleges and universities in South Korea in 2008, serving more than 3.5 million students and employing more than 70,000 faculty.[5] The sheer size of the college market was too large for Kim and Andes to ignore.

In Third Place

With the possible exception of Starbucks, the other largest sellers of coffee in the United States—7-Eleven, Dunkin Donuts, and McDonald's—were not really places that customers lingered. They bought their coffee, often via the drive-through, and then exited the store. Europeans and most Latin Americans lingered: Drinking coffee was a cultural experience, not just the caffeine fix that it was for most in the United States.

Koreans are a mix of the two coffee shop culture types. The hectic pace of life in the big cities means late nights and early mornings. Coffee is what helps get Koreans to work on time and to stay awake in the afternoon; however, coffee shops are often referred to in Korea as the *third place*: Your home is where your family is; work is where you earn a living with your colleagues; the coffee shop is the third place—an escape from the pressures of the other two.

Korea is one of the most wired countries in the world in terms of broadband Internet access, so Koreans do not need to go to a coffee shop to find a Wi-Fi hot spot. The coffee shop is instead a place to meet friends, do some homework, get out of the rain or into the air conditioning, and enjoy a modern, comfortable environment for an hour or more—all for the price of a pretty good cup of coffee. Lee Min-Kyu, strategy manager for Starbucks Coffee Korea, described the coffee shop setting:

> When a customer enters the store, he or she is first greeted by the aroma of high-quality roasted coffee, the taste is just as great, the seats are comfortable, the interior decor is appealing to eye, and the music being played is a delight to the ear. In this way, the customer can feel satisfaction through each of the five senses.[6]

Poring Over the Numbers

Naver, Korea's most popular Web portal, listed 740 different coffee brands just in Seoul as of July 2010.[7] Many—perhaps most—of these had only a single location and were located around Seoul's many college campuses: That is simply the supply of the free market being created to meet demand. Virtually all of Korea's other business-to-consumer (B2C) vertical markets—including bakeries, bookstores, convenience, department and discount stores, family restaurants, fast-food restaurants, gas stations, movie theaters, and pizza places—were dominated by no more than six players: often just three or four. What is it about coffee that allows for so much success by so many large brands? Low cost of entry and few barriers to entry are the easy answers, but you do not see this number of brands with more than 50 locations in any other Korean B2C vertical in which similar factors exist (see Table 3.1).

Table 3.1 Coffee Shop Brands in South Korea with More Than 50 Locations

Brand	Country of Origin	Number of Outlets*	First Store Opened
Ediya	Korea	370	2001
Starbucks	USA	329	1999
Angel-in-Us	Korea	310	2000
Rosebud	Korea	250	2001
Hollys	Korea	227	1998
Coffee Bean	USA	213	2001
Tom n Toms	Korea	175	2004
Sleepless in Seattle	Korea	107	2004
Davinci	Korea	105	2000
Caffe Bene	Korea	100	2009
Pascucci	Korea	71	2001
Twosome Place	Korea	68	2002
Seven Monkeys	Korea	50+	2006ᵢ

*Estimate of current stores and confirmed 2010 openings as of July 2010.
Source: Corporate Web sites.

Another explanation for so many brands with so many locations is that Koreans are loyal customers, as they tend to patronize the same coffee shop brand rather than just choose whatever coffee shop is closest; therefore, a given brand needs to be everywhere. The tendency for loyalty is further accentuated by what can only be described as Koreans' obsession with loyalty cards, often called *mileage cards* by Koreans even when they are not issued by airlines. These cards are the physical part of programs that reward customers for frequenting the same brand over and over again. Virtually everyone in Korea has a wallet full of cards that earn cash, points, or offer a discount of some kind. Even small coffee houses have the *buy-10-get-one-free* punch cards of a less-digital era. Current academic research suggests, "Coffee has shed its status as an item of personal preference and has instead become an essential part of the Korean palate. ... The average age of Korea's coffee consumers was 32, which indicates that the popularity of coffee is no longer confined to the younger generation."[8]

The battle to be number one among the high-end cafés (thus excluding Ediya and Rosebud) was ongoing. Starbucks' joint venture partner in Korea was Shinsegae, an upscale department store chain with hotel interests. Lotte owned Angel-in-Us and competed with Shinsegae in the department store space. Angel-in-Us had been growing faster than Starbucks in terms of number of locations and perhaps had an advantage in that it also owned Lotteria, a popular quick service restaurant similar in some ways to McDonald's. Lotte arguably had more experience than Shinsegae in marketing food and coffee to Koreans. Starbucks led Angel-in-Us in the number of Korean locations by a margin of 188 to 50 in 2006, but that lead was expected to narrow to 329 to 310 by the end of 2010.[9] Starbucks, however, retained a big lead in terms of gross revenue,[10] suggesting that Starbucks customers spent more on average than those at Angel-in-Us (see Table 3.2). Lee Min-Kyu commented on Starbucks' growth:

Our store program is completely customer driven. The number of stores that we will open depends completely on demand as expressed by the customer. Some may say there are already a lot of Starbucks stores right now, but we don't agree; the Korean coffee market is enormous so we will continue to open more.[11]

Table 3.2 Price of a Caffe Americano*

Brand	Price	Web Site
Coffee Bean	4,500	www.coffeebeankorea.com/
Angel-in-Us	4,100	www.angelinus.co.kr/
Pascucci	3,800	www.caffe-pascucci.co.kr/
Twosome Place	3,800	www.twosomeplace.co.kr/
Caffe Bene	3,600	www.caffebene.co.kr/main/
Starbucks	3,600	www.istarbucks.co.kr/
Hollys	3,500	www.hollys.co.kr/
Seven Monkeys	3,500	www.sevenmonkeys.co.kr/
Tom n Toms	3,300	http://tomntoms.com/
Davinci	3,300	www.edavinci.co.kr/web/main.htm
Sleepless in Seattle	2,800 (Daegu)	www.siscoffee.com/
Ediya	2,800	www.ediya.com/
Rosebud	2,000	www.irosebud.co.kr/

*Data current as of July 2010 for a regular size cup.

Source: Empirical. Priced in South Korean Won as of July 2010 (US$1 = ~KRW1,200).

According to the U.S. Commercial Service in Seoul, U.S. franchises were sought after in Korea, but several challenges remained:

[P]otential Korean franchisees are often reluctant to pay the relatively high franchising fees and royalties required by U.S. headquarters. Other common franchising requirements, such as minimum facility size and the required number of store openings within a certain period are often very challenging for Korean franchisers to meet.[12]

The market was still dynamic: A 2002 U.S. Commercial Service report, "Coffee Franchises Booming in Korea," accurately predicted that "growing demand for high-quality coffee among Koreans and their enthusiastic embrace of foreign fashions and trends [means that] coffee franchise opportunities in Korea are rapidly expanding."[13] Of the 16 brands highlighted in the report, only five were still active in the Korean market eight years later.

Has the Cup Runneth Over?

The local coffee market is defying expectations and seems to be still in the midst of growth. Then again, spending 4,000 Won on a cup of coffee is not a bad choice when you are looking for a place to meet someone for several hours.[14]

—Marketing representative from Coffee Bean Korea

Korean companies often provided lots of useful marketing data on their Web sites; the financial information that publicly traded companies in the United States made available was not always complete, but you could generally find the history of the company, store openings on an annual basis, menus, and current promotions. Visiting the Web sites after having visited the stores also helped Kim and Andes get more of a feel for each brand and their messaging. If they went with an existing brand, they wanted one that seemed modern, sophisticated, and experienced in the digital age.

Starbucks and Coffee Bean could be taken off the prospect list immediately: Both local parent companies owned all the local stores (see Table 3.3). Angel-in-Us was owned by a large Korean conglomerate, which struck Kim and Andes as unlikely to be flexible in letting them make any changes or bring their respective core competencies to bear. Sleepless in Seattle had yet to come to Seoul: Was a local master franchising agreement for the capital city possible? If so, could Kim and Andes obtain the rights to diversify the nearly nonexistent menu and logo products to suit a wealthier and more diverse market than the brand's hometown of Daegu? Franchisors were generally very reluctant to do this, other than change some minor menu localization when operating in a new country; for example, the Outback Steakhouses all over South Korea served kimchi, something you would not find on the menu in Alabama. That was one of the key benefits of franchising: The franchisor gave the franchisee a proven model that only required operational execution for the franchise to be successful. Kim and Andes believed that business as usual in this crowded market would not be successful with so late an entry.

Table 3.3 Possibility of Franchising Major Korean Coffee Shops Brands

Brand	Franchising Available?	Comment
Angel-in-Us	No	Owned by Lotte, a large Korean conglomerate
Caffe Bene	Yes	—
Coffee Bean	No	All stores owned by Coffee Bean Korea
Davinci	Yes	—
Ediya	Yes	—
Hollys	Yes	—
Pascucci	Yes	—
Rosebud	Yes	Takeout only (no seating)
Seven Monkeys	Yes	Japanese brand
Sleepless in Seattle	Yes	Started in Daegu, South Korea
Starbucks	No	All stores owned by Starbucks Korea
Tom n Toms	Yes	—
Twosome Place	No	Owned by CJ, a large Korean conglomerate

Kim and Andes wrestled with this conundrum: What mattered more in a crowded maturing market—brand or differentiation? If the answer was brand, then franchising was clearly the preferred mode of entry for them. If the answer was differentiation, a new concept was needed. As it was, the coffee shops mostly differentiated themselves based on the food they served (see Table 3.4). Was there a new, creative menu that a new coffee shop could offer to attract customers? What about fresh-roasted coffee instead of preroasted like all the big players offered? Perhaps they could sell wine and coffee, or Irish coffees with full-strength whiskey mixed in. Kim and Andes did not want to turn their coffee shop into a bar: Could they sell alcohol without the shop feeling like a bar? Or what about coffee and English education (e.g., magazines, games, online exercises) focused on the student market?

Table 3.4 Food Available at Major Korean Coffee Shops

Brand	Food
Angel-in-Us	Sandwiches, bagels, waffles, pastries, chocolate
Caffe Bene	Gelato, waffles
Coffee Bean	Cookies, bagels, cakes, muffins, scones
Davinci	Bread, cookies, bagels, cakes, muffins, sandwiches
Ediya	Waffles, cookies, bagels, cakes, muffins, pretzels
Hollys	Waffles, cookies, bagels, cakes, muffins, scones
Pascucci	Cake, paninis, bagels
Rosebud	Pie, cake, cookies
Seven Monkeys	Cookies, bagels, cakes, muffins
Sleepless in Seattle	Cheesecake, flatbread pizza (at some locations)
Starbucks	Cake, cookies, pastries, sandwiches, bagels, chocolate
Tom n Toms	Wide variety of pretzels, bread
Twosome Place	Cake, cookies, muffins, sandwiches, bagels

The path was clear to Kim and Andes: The first decision was the mode of entry. If the decision was made to franchise, that would resolve most of the other issues. It was tempting to go the franchising route and get instant brand value in a country where brands were important. If the decision was to go it alone, then product differentiation based on location(s), target market, menu, and theme would be the challenge. Could they use their academic credentials to boost their brand? This seemed more fun to Kim and Andes. Perhaps they could open their first shop on a campus and thus avoid land

and construction costs in exchange for a revenue-sharing agreement with the university. If so, less than US$100,000 might be enough, and they could self-finance. This seemed like something that could be repeated on multiple campuses, with cash flow from existing shops funding the debt needed to open subsequent shops. Perhaps there would even come a time when others would pay them a franchise fee to expand their idea. With the cold green goodness of their kiwi smoothies almost gone on a hot summer day, the two went to work to develop a strategy.

Endnotes

1. Central Intelligence Agency, "The World Factbook," https://www.cia.gov/library/publications/the-world-factbook/geos/ks.html (accessed August 14, 2010).

2. Ibid.

3. Forbes.com, "The World's Leading Companies," www.forbes.com/lists/2010/18/global-2000-10_The-Global-2000_Counrty.html (accessed August 14, 2010).

4. Bziuk, J, "Understanding the Korean Workplace Through the Eyes of a Foreigner" (unpublished master's thesis, Warsaw University, 2010).

5. Kim, Young-Chul, "Universalization of Tertiary Education," Korean Educational Development Institute, Seoul, 2008, p. 13; http://eng.kedi.re.kr/09_edu/img/koredu/2.Universalization%20of%20Teritary%20Education.PDF (accessed August 14, 2010).

6. Duerden, Charles, "Wake Up and Smell the Coffee," *Invest Korea*, May–June 2006; www.ikjournal.com/InvestKoreaWar/work/journal/content/content_print.jsp?code=4440216 (accessed August 14, 2010).

7. Conversation with a Korean Ministry of Trade official in July 2010.

8. Hyung-Seok Lee and Min-Sun Yeu, "Factors Influencing the Intention to Redeem Coffee Shop Coupons in Korea," *International Journal of Business and Management*, Vol. 5, No. 7 (July 2010): 95; www.ccsenet.org/journal/index.php/ijbm/article/viewFile/6627/5235 (accessed August 14, 2010).

9. Financial News, "Shinsegae or Lotte, Who Will Be the Winner of the Battle of Coffee in 2010?" *Financial News*, July 7, 2010; www.fnnews.com/view?ra=Sent0701m_View&corp=fnnews&arcid=100706222755&cDateYear=2010&cDateMonth=07&cDateDay=07 (accessed August 14, 2010).

10. Ibid.

11. Duerden, Charles, "Wake Up and Smell the Coffee," *Invest Korea*, May–June 2006; www.ikjournal.com/InvestKoreaWar/work/journal/content/content_print.jsp?code=4440216 (accessed August 14, 2010).

12. U.S. Commercial Service, "Doing Business in Korea: A Country Commercial Guide for U.S. Companies," 2010; www.buyusa.gov/korea/en/ccg2010.doc (accessed August 14, 2010).

13. Sung, Grace, "Coffee Franchises Booming in Korea," *International Market Insight: Korea*, Published by the U.S. Commercial Service, 2002.

14. Tong-Hyung Kim, "Too Many Cafes?," *The Korea Times*, December 12, 2009; www.koreatimes.co.kr/www/news/biz/2010/05/123_56859.html (accessed on July 12, 2010).

4

International Marketing and Franchising at Marks & Spencer

Ilan Alon

For years, M&S had used a simple marketing philosophy: Produce high-quality products under a recognized brand name at affordable (but not low) prices, and advertise through word of mouth. However, this marketing philosophy has come under attack as the company's competitive edge has eroded. The move to develop a marketing department was a departure from a long tradition of ignoring marketing in favor of a product-oriented corporate culture. The problem facing James Benfield, named marketing director in 1998 after a 28-year career at M&S, was a serious one: how to help M&S emerge from the slump and reposition itself as a fierce global competitor in the international marketplace?

Brief Company Background

Marks & Spencer of Britain (often referred to as Marks & Sparks by locals) is a general retailer that sells clothes, gifts, home furnishings, and foods under the St. Michael trademark in the UK, Europe, the Americas, and the Far East. The company also operates a financial services segment, which accounted for some 3% of the company's 1998 profits.[1]

Marks & Spencer (M&S) started as a stall in 1884 by Michael Marks in the Leeds market using a £5 loan from a wholesaler. From its inception, the company stressed value and low prices as a hallmark

49

for development. By 1901, the company had acquired 35 outlets as well as a new partner, Tom Spencer. By 1949, all the company's stores carried mostly private label (St. Michael) products produced by British suppliers.[2]

For many years, the company's mission had been to offer consumers quality, value, and service. The company relied on five operating principles to achieve its mission:

1. Developing long-term relationships with suppliers
2. Providing value through a narrow merchandise selection at affordable prices
3. Supporting local (British) industry[3]
4. Promoting from within[4]
5. Using the St. Michael branding for most of its products[5]

These operating tenets have gained M&S the support of British producers, consumers, and workers. The sixth largest employer in British manufacturing, the textile industry, with over 354,000 workers, owes a large part of its existence to M&S.[6] M&S has encouraged British textile manufacturers to keep factories at home, leading to tighter quality control and more flexibility in manufacturing and distribution.[7] The British have responded with affection. A British writer described M&S as a "quintessential British institution, woven into the fabric of our national life, as firmly lodged in our psyches as furniture in the front room."[8]

Business Situation

Using the business model described above, M&S had achieved impressive growth rates and market shares in many of its business segments. By 1994, the firm had 18% of the UK retail market, 33% of the women's undergarment market, and 20% of the men's suit market.[9]

By the late 1990s, the company had 40% of the nation's underwear market and 14% of the clothing market—the only retailer in Europe to (then) have double-digit market share.[10] M&S's food market share was then 4.3%.[11] These impressive market shares had gained M&S its reputation as a leading retailer in the United Kingdom.

The euphoria, however, did not last, as M&S caught investors and business spectators off guard. In 1998, the company's stock price slipped 34%.[12] Pretax profits fell by as much as 41% (to $1.09 billion) and market share declined, for the first time in years, by almost 1%.[13] In May 1999, the company reported full-year profits of £630 million, a 50% fall from 1997 to 1998.[14] Warburg Dillon Read, an investment bank, reduced its profit expectations for M&S by 10% for 1999–2000.[15]

Overseas profits declined from their 1996–1997 high of £100 million to a loss of £15 million, before exceptional items, for fiscal year 1998.[16] Sales measured in local currencies were down by 3%.[17]

Table 4.1 represents a financial snapshot of the company, comparing key financial measures of M&S (Britain's leading retailer) with those of Wal-Mart (the leading retailer in the United States) at the time.[18]

Table 4.1 Financial Snapshot of Marks & Spencer*

	Marks & Spencer	**Wal-Mart**
Market capitalization	$18 billion	$204 billion
Revenue	$14 billion	$144 billion
Return on assets	13%	10%
Return on equity	18%	23%
Current ratio	0.98	1.30
Price-earnings ratio	31	44
52-week price trend	-31%	63%

*Compiled by the author from 1999 Dow Jones Industrial and Market Guide data.

The company blamed consumer confidence and a strong pound for the decline in sales and company value. An M&S Press Release in 1999 stated that the deterioration in 1998–1999 profits had been the result of (1) a shortfall in expected sales, (2) a slowdown in overseas markets, and (3) the purchase of Littlewoods stores for £90 million. A recessionary business environment in Europe and the Asian crisis had put a great strain on global profitability. At the same time, domestic and international competition had intensified both from specialty retailers and mega-merchandisers, such as Wal-Mart.

But stockholders and business analysts were not convinced that the company's problems were merely external. M&S stock was underperforming other British retailers by more than 25%. Some blamed M&S management for dull merchandising, poor inventory control, and slow responses to competitive environmental conditions.[19] Industry commentators criticized the color, size, and shape of their clothes; the poor retailing climate; the unglamorous stores; the overpriced products; and the lack of personal service.[20]

Competition

The core values of M&S—quality, affordability, and service—came under the greatest attack not from critics, but from competitors. Retailers such as Top Shop, Kookai, Miss Selfridge, Jigsaw, Oasis, Warehouse, and The Gap offered more fashionable designs and trendier labels. Other retailers, such as Next, Debenhams, and BhS, offered better values. Food chains, such as Tesco, Waitrose, and Sainsbury's, had moved more fully into prepared foods.[21] M&S was being challenged in every one of its business segments. By its own admission, M&S had not changed quickly enough to react to accelerating competition, which had resulted in an unacceptable fall in profitability and market share.[22]

Marketing at Marks & Spencer

Products

M&S products can be divided into three lines of business: (1) general merchandise, (2) foods, and (3) financial services. General merchandise includes clothing, undergarments, handbags, footwear, goods for the home, children's toys, books, and cosmetics.

The food business offers a wide range of prepared foods, perishables, ethnic foods, meats, and beverages, both alcoholic and not. Among the eclectic selection of foods are chocolate-covered ginger biscuits, salmon *en croute*, chicken tikka sandwiches, and mushroom risotto.[23] Perhaps an example of the bridge M&S is building from its traditional image of itself as retailer to the upper middle classes, the food segment's upscale offerings extended even further as food offerings with new bistro style meals and juice and coffee bars were introduced in some stores.[24]

Finally, the company also sells financial services, including secured store credit cards, personal loans, personal equity plans, unit trusts, and life insurance. M&S created a core of business for its own credit cards by refusing to honor other widely held cards, such as MasterCard, Visa, Discover, or American Express. As an inducement, and to offset any negative effects of this policy, customers who deposit money into their M&S credit card accounts receive up to 20 times the purchasing power of their deposits. For example, with a deposit of $100, the customer gets a line of credit of $2000.[25] The company has also diversified into life insurances and group pension contracts.[26] Although the financial-services segment is relatively small (about 3% of profits), it is the fastest growing segment of M&S's operations. Profits in 1998 increased 24% to £111 million, while the number of card accounts increased to 5.2 million.[27]

Throughout its history, M&S has increasingly relied upon the St. Michael brand name to deliver its image to consumers. Because M&S's expertise has traditionally been its ability to consistently deliver high-quality products, the St. Michael tag has become synonymous with that expertise, and has allowed M&S to target core sectors of its demographic market: children and middle-class housewives. This overreliance upon one (house) brand, however, has not gone unchallenged in the wake of the plunge in value after 1997. A commentator in the *Financial Times* suggested in 1999 that the company follow the example of Debenhams (a competing retailer) and use sub-brands to target specific segments of its market.[28]

Price

Marks & Spencer had followed a value-price strategy from its inception, starting with Michael Marks, who put all his products for a penny on one side of the store with a sign saying "Don't ask the price, it's a penny." Because M&S had historically concentrated on middle-class customers, it had never reevaluated its value-pricing strategy. Although most of its suppliers were from Britain, which has higher textile manufacturing costs than some developing nations, M&S had been able to maintain its value by developing strong economic bonds with suppliers. Through its economies of scale in buying, M&S had been able to require manufacturers to adhere to strict quality standards and to bargain for lower prices for its customers.[29]

However, due to the strength of the pound sterling, this high proportion of homegrown products had led to a substantially lower profit margin in the mid-to-late 1990s. Still, M&S had held the line on prices even while its margins decreased, remaining moderately priced relative to its European competitors.

In anticipation of the Euro conversion, since the late 1990s the company has featured prices both in local currency and Euros in its European stores. It also has limited conversion tables by the cashiers. As it looks to the future, the conceptual change evident in Euro-Pound unit pricing may well herald an increasing willingness to become international in its suppliers as well as its clientele.

Place

M&S stores come in two basic formats: a general merchandise store, with its basement dedicated to foods, or a store that offers foods only. The average size of the store ranges from 35,000 to 40,000 square feet (3,252 to 3,716 square meters), with a minimum of 100,000 square feet (9,290 square meters) for remote locations. In recent years, the firm has been aggressively increasing the square footage of its stores.[30]

According to its 1998 Annual Report, M&S tries to locate its stores on the main streets of major cities, claiming that it seeks "to build critical mass around capital cities or across important conurbation, such as the Rhine-Ruhr area in Germany."[31] For example, Paris, the most significant market in Europe, hosts 20% of the country's population and 10 out of the 20 M&S stores in the country. The company owns a very valuable global portfolio of property, with footholds in prime cities and districts across the world.[32] Competition for prime space, however, has made it necessary to locate in more remote locations.

In 1994, M&S started to focus aggressively on building distribution networks to supply its growing global operations.[33] The focal point of this network, however, has remained in the United Kingdom.

Promotion

M&S has tended to avoid media advertising in favor of the powerful, cost-effective traditional tendencies of word of mouth and social cachet. As we observed when looking at product diversity, the ubiquity of the St. Michael label has allowed M&S to connect to its customer base over a broad segment of products. The implied quality of the brand has served the firm well, promoting consumption while spurring cycles of word of mouth and copycat purchasing. Yet, the success of the St. Michael's brand has led to a blinkered vision of the benefits to be gained from the marketing support popular brand names generate. As in the case of its supply chain, an overreliance on one aspect has tended to create a *cul de sac* for the firm.

In the past, the company had used advertising only in rare cases, such as when M&S was introducing a new product or retail format or when brand-name recognition was low, as in the case of its store introduction in Paris.[34] The media budget was £4.7 million in 1998, compared with the £18.8 million of 10 other leading retailers.[35] After a succession of disappointing financial statements, the company significantly increased its advertising budget to approximately £20 million.[36] The company had already invited advertising agencies to pitch and planned its second-ever television campaign, geared toward a focus on M&S products.[37]

Internationalization of Marks & Spencer

M&S experimental involvement with internationalization began in the 1940s. Unlike most service firms, however, the company began exporting its St. Michael brands overseas as a way to test the waters. (The company did not and does not own manufacturers; it merely brands merchandise using the St. Michael private label.) Researchers have estimated that in 1955 the company was exporting about $1,146,000 worth of merchandise.[38]

The early internationalization of the company was mostly due to domestic factors. Internally, the company felt that it had saturated the domestic market and that expansion would have to come from overseas. Externally, some Labor Party members were suggesting nationalizing the leading domestic retailers.[39] Internationalization was seen as a tool of diversification.

Some international franchising relationships were formed as a result of the export businesses' activities. Importers of the St. Michael brand, familiar with the success of the brand in their countries, also bought the business format (including store layout and operating style) from M&S. By the early 1990s, St. Michael franchises were operating in 14 economies, including those with ties to the Commonwealth, such as Gibraltar, Bermuda, Israel, and the Philippines.[40] Franchising allowed the company to achieve a global presence with minimal economic and political risks. As M&S's familiarity with internationalization grew, more direct modes of entry, such as acquisitions and joint ventures, were used. By 1996, the company had 645 outlets worldwide, most of which (58%) were in the UK, Europe, and Canada.[41]

Modes of Entry

The internationalization of M&S resembles the theoretical explanations of service firm internationalization.[42] These theories suggest that service firms look to international expansion as they gain experience, and experience a subsequent willingness to commit more company resources and take additional risks. Retailers will tend to use relatively less-risky modes of entry, such as exporting and franchising, in markets where market and political risk are high. Retailers will tend to share ownership where sole ownership is prohibited or restricted. In markets with significant per capita purchasing power, large populations, and developed infrastructures—such as in the United States and Europe—retailers are more willing to enter through high-control, high-risk modes of entry, such as sole ownership and acquisition.

M&S utilizes various modes of entry around the world. The company believes in opening its own stores and expanding through acquisitions in major economies. On the other hand, M&S has expanded through franchise agreements into countries where a partner's local expertise is viewed as beneficial, according to their 1998 Annual Report.[43] The company owns stores in Belgium, Canada, France,

Germany, Hong Kong, Ireland, Spain, and the Netherlands; there are franchises in countries such as the Bahamas, Bermuda, Canary Islands, Cyprus, the Czech Republic, Gibraltar, and Israel.[44]

When forming international alliances, M&S has often preferred an experienced retailer with significant market share. In 1990, M&S went into its first joint venture with Cortefiel, one of Spain's leading retailers. A joint venture was initially used in Spain because it was felt that the market knowledge and power of an existing retailer would help mitigate the problems of cultural distance and of the sometimes-adverse political climate.[45] In Australia, M&S chose a partner who was an experienced local clothing retailer. In China, the company is looking for a likely candidate as the industrial structure of the economy develops.[46]

Maureen Whitehead was one of the first researchers to examine international franchising at M&S.[47] Whitehead's research revealed that M&S used a franchise format that was a hybrid between first-trademark franchising and business-format franchising. She proposed that the company used franchising in countries that had relatively small populations or low per capita incomes but were sufficiently promising as markets to warrant a small number of stores.

Trade name franchising is based on the supply of merchandise and trademarks, such as gas service stations and automobile dealerships, while business format franchising relies on the transfer of a formalized operating style. M&S's franchisees need to show short- and medium-horizon business plans and demonstrate a minimum level of turnover. The franchisee pays through merchandise purchases and a percentage of inventory turnover. Franchisees can pick selectively from the M&S inventory, instead of being forced to carry the full range of products available through the British-owned stores.

Regional Analysis of M&S Internationalization

A truly global firm should have operations in all three regional economic blocks. Since 1975, M&S has increasingly become a global retailer, with a presence in each of the major trading blocks: the Americas, Europe, and the Far East. Table 4.2 shows current operating results and comparisons of the three regions.

Table 4.2 Operating Results and Regional Comparisons

	The Americas	Europe°	Far East
Turnover	606	538	128
Operating profits	17	33	18
Number of stores	43	53	10
(Franchised)	(5)°°	(15)	(33)

°Includes some Middle-Eastern states
°°Not including Brooks Brothers (119) and Kings Supermarkets (22)
Source: M&S Annual Report 1998

The Americas

The first major round of acquisitions for M&S occurred in 1973 with the purchases of Canadian People's Department Stores (a budget retailer), D'Allaird's (which marketed to mature women), and Walker's store (modeled after British M&S's own format). Canada was seen by M&S's executives to be a low-risk investment because of its high per capita incomes, solid infrastructure, large middle class, low political risk, and the predominance of English as both linguistic and cultural currency. Because they perceived little cultural distance, they transferred their business formula almost unchanged from the United Kingdom to Canada. They quickly found that even Canada required some modifications. The presumption that M&S would flourish without modifying itself to fit the cultural environment was one that would plague the firm.

After initially disappointing sales after entrance into the market, the Canadian stores were customized to suit local needs by increasing the amount of Canadian merchandise, enlarging food departments, restructuring inner-city stores, and opening suburban stores—rejigging that was generally new to the M&S experience. The changes were made too slowly and, by 1988, the stores had lost about $7 million. Thereafter, the D'Allaird's stores were closed to cut costs and to focus the corporate gaze on more profitable operations.[48] In May 1999, M&S announced, as reported by *Dow Jones*, that it would be closing all 38 M&S stores in Canada by September 1999.[49] In a press release that same year, the company reported that it had decided that Canada no longer fit the strategic future, several attempts to return it to profit having failed.[50] The cost of withdrawal is estimated at £25 million.

M&S entered the United States in 1988 using a similar strategy to the Canadian one, through acquisitions. It bought Brooks Brothers (department store, nicknamed Brooks Bros.) to market its clothes and Kings Supermarket to sell its food line. Unlike M&S, which bought its supplies, these companies owned manufacturing facilities. The formats of these stores are consistent with, if not identical to, the essential formats of the two models M&S employs. Brooks Brothers did not have a basement facility in which it sells food, nor did it sell general items.

After the acquisition, Brooks Brothers (M&S largest operation in the Americas) expanded its sports' selection, widened its product base, and enlarged its customer base. It opened a few locations in malls targeting a younger market. The company used some products from the Brooks Brothers clothing line to sell in its UK and European stores. M&S did not change the names of the U.S. chains, probably unwilling to toy with their loyal customer bases, nor did it significantly change the product offerings.

The purchase of Brooks Brothers contributed to continuing innovation in the merchandise mix, offered M&S an opportunity to compete in the largest economy in the world, and gave M&S a foothold in the Far East. While some believed that the purchase of Brooks Brothers was overpriced (30 times 1987 profits), it provided M&S with 21 joint venture stores with Daido Worsted Mills in Japan, three U.S.-based factories, a charge card business, and a direct marketing operation.[51]

For the year ending 1998, Brooks Brothers increased its number of stores by 7 (to 119), increased its market share of the U.S. men's clothing market, improved direct marketing, and invested in a new warehouse management system to increase service efficiency. The M&S 1998 Annual Report noted that the chain expected to become more contemporary, broaden its market appeal (particularly to working women), and modernize its brand image. Commentary in that same year noted that Kings Supermarkets had also shown satisfactory results; two new stores were added in New Jersey, and new stores were being pioneered in Florham Park, located in one of New York City's outer boroughs. Five new Kings Supermarkets were expected to open in 1999, according to the Annual Report.

Europe

M&S entered the European market in 1975, less than two years after the soon-to-be disastrous Canadian acquisitions. France was chosen as the gateway country, and Paris was chosen as the gateway city to the rest of Europe.[52] Unlike Canada, it was understood that a great deal of market research would be needed if they were to thrive in the contentious Gallic market. The company decided to adapt the store to French reality by offering snugger fits to its clothing, a wide selection of French wines, and fewer British imports. Due to a lack of brand-name recognition, the company also relied on advertising to spark interest in the stores.[53] From there, M&S expanded to Belgium (1975), Spain (1990), Germany (1996), and more recently to smaller economies, including Greece, Hungary, Portugal, and the Czech Republic.

The European section of the 1998 Annual Report includes report-age of Eastern and Western Europe and some states in the Middle East, noting that M&S is seeking to increase customization to local national tastes by adding brand names to the already successful St. Michael brand. In Europe, the company owns 37 stores (in France, Belgium, Holland, Spain, Germany, and Ireland) and franchises 53 stores across the rest of Europe and the Middle East. M&S plans to open new stores in Spain, Belgium, Holland, and Ireland; develop new franchises in Turkey, Dubai, and Poland; and increase square footage in the Czech Republic, Greece, and Cyprus. The company had hoped to have 60 stores in Continental Europe by the year 2000.[54] Still, about 80% of the stock sold in continental Europe is the same as the UK home market, while the other 20% reflects differences in culture, size, climate, and local preferences.[55]

In Europe, sales from core stores and recently expanded stores were below expectations for 1998–1999, particularly in the major economies of France, Germany, and Spain. Corporate press releases at the time noted that profit margins had deteriorated as the company attempted to maintain good value; sales in the Middle East, on the other hand, were particularly strong, especially in a new operation in Kuwait. To increase the profitability of European operations, the company (1) closed unprofitable stores (in Zaragosa and Parinor), (2) acquired full control of the Spanish business, (3) gave more control to local managers, and (4) developed a European buying department to meet local demand.

Far East

The entry into the Far East was twofold. M&S's first exposure to business in the Far East occurred indirectly through the purchase of Brooks Brothers (1988), which co-owned affiliates in Japan. Building upon Brooks Brothers' 19+ years of brand-exposure trading experi-ence with Japan, M&S opened two new franchises in the Hong Kong market in 1998. M&S believes that Asia will be a major market for

Brooks Brothers because of the region's receptiveness to U.S. culture and because so much of the foreign value system (in terms of one's attempt to buy the culture by buying the clothing, e.g.) is bound up in the prestige factor of the commodities presented, according to the company's 1998 Annual Report. However, a 1999 press release observed that Brooks Brothers Japan had been adversely affected by recent recessionary conditions in the economy.[56]

Using the M&S brand name allowed the firm its second market penetration. By keying on the brand-name perception of its high(er) quality Western-style items, those customers prone to buying European styles have created the potential future base for internationalization at the store level. The stores that M&S opened in Hong Kong, which were supplied through the British home base, are the result of this strategy. All of the wholly owned stores in the Far East are in Hong Kong; the 33 other outlets are franchised across six other nations in the region. In recent years, the company has expanded to suburban areas of Hong Kong, a move it believes will help it penetrate the Chinese market.[57] The company already has a resident office in Shanghai whose purpose is to evaluate the market and to spark interest in a joint venture there.[58] Subsequently, the company expanded its presence in Thailand, the Philippines, Indonesia, Korea, and Australia, as M&S reported in its 1998 Annual Report.

M&S stores were not exempted from the 1997 Asian economic crisis, which had a dramatic effect on all retail sales in the region. Despite the slowdown, the company was able to increase the number of owned and franchised stores by 9 to 43. The 1998 Annual Report and contemporaneous press releases reported that the company's expansion and the adverse conditions created by the Asian crisis had hampered sales and profitability in Asia, and that no new development was planned for the (then) near future. Rather, the company planned to source locally and buy temporarily depressed properties. Hong Kong would remain a strategic base, despite sales being £20 million below expectations for 1998–1999.

Problems Identified by Industry Observers

According to popular magazines such as *Business Week* and the *Economist*, M&S's international marketing challenges fall into three broad categories: (1) overreliance on the British market, (2) top management's internal orientation, and (3) corporate culture.

Overreliance on the British Market

M&S has relied too much on the British market both for its customers and its suppliers, exposing the company to unsystematic risk. The British market constitutes 85% of sales and 94% of profits. The reduction in profits of 23% in 289 stores in Britain is largely what led to depressed stock prices in 1998.[59]

M&S's insistence on buying its clothes from domestic manufacturers—a policy that gained it support from its citizenry, but not necessarily its customers—has been problematic. Approximately 65% of all products sold in M&S stores were manufactured in the UK, according to a 1999 press release. This dependence on British suppliers has limited the scope of its product offerings and innovations, led to deterioration of its competitive position *vis-à-vis* retailers, which import cheaper garments from abroad, and made its exported products expensive in relation to world markets.[60]

The insistence on buying British produced goods has also been unhealthy for M&S's suppliers. In response to the M&S slowdown of the late 1990s, suppliers had to cut almost 2,300 jobs. The company broke with tradition in 1999 and started to encourage suppliers to manufacture overseas.[61] The need to lower global production and distribution costs is a key problem requiring attention.

Ironically, given the difficulties it has occasionally encountered overseas, M&S needs to internationalize even more than it has to further diversify the risk of a downturn in any one economy. *Business*

Week suggested in 1998 that M&S reduce its dependence on the local British market and continue its international expansion.[62] However, additional international expansion would require great resource commitment, a difficult task during hard economic times. Furthermore, as developed countries become saturated and highly competitive markets, retailers will need to expand to increasingly risky markets, including countries where substantial cultural, economic, and political differences exist. Two core obstacles, requiring much forethought but crucial to success in internationalization, are the choice of host country and the mode of entry decisions.

Top Management's Internal Orientation

A 1998 article in the *Economist* observed that top management and the board of governors at M&S had been inward looking for too long.[63] The board was then made up of no less than 16 executives—most of whom were career M&S employees—and 6 nonexecutives, including one each from the two cofounding families. The author(s) argued, "With M&S now selling financial services and going overseas, the narrowness of experience of M&S's senior managers and board directors is a weakness."

The narrowness of top-management experience was also reflected in the choice of a chief executive to replace Richard Greenbury. Keith Oates, who joined M&S in 1984 as finance director, having built a career with blue-chip companies, lost the top job to Peter Salsbury, who joined the company in 1970 fresh out of London School of Economics.[64]

The new marketing director, James Benfield, himself a 28-year M&S veteran, originally joined M&S as a graduate trainee.[65] Despite his stated desire for new marketing input, his four newly appointed managers for each store type are also M&S employees.[66] M&S resembled Sears in that it had been inward looking for too long. It was not unreasonable to see a connection between corporate culture and the depressed stock prices of both companies.[67]

The international orientation of top management at any given firm will tend to be the function of four variables: cultural distance, levels of education, proficiency in foreign languages, and international experiences. These factors will inevitably influence the decision-making matrices of management, and an awareness of these variables has been shown to be an important internal factor of internationalization.[68] M&S's top management personnel and board of directors were mostly white, British-born, British-educated males who had spent the majority of their careers at M&S, surrounded by the like-minded.

Corporate Culture

M&S corporate culture had always been of the top-down type. Decision making was (and is) centralized, and the company ruled from the top through command and control. Prices, products, colors, and even designs had to be approved at the top. "Those who were close to the customer weren't listened to or encouraged to be bold and take risks."[69] Although the company used famous designers, such as Paul Smith, Betty Jackson, and Ghost, it never used their names in promotions, nor did it give them much latitude in designing new fashions; in fact, the prevailing attitude was that "we know best."[70]

This core attitude circulated throughout many of its business practices. For example, the company accepted only M&S credit cards in its British stores, used very limited advertising, and insisted on buying British textiles. However, M&S's old business model does not fit the new realities of the global marketplace. Competitors struggle for market share by offering increasingly better quality, nicer service, lower prices, and more pleasant shopping experiences. The result is a stepladder of increasing customer expectations that are more difficult to satisfy. Companies that cannot keep up with the pace of change will eventually perish. M&S's famous quality and service had not kept pace with the modern notions of these terms.[71]

The Problem

Notwithstanding any journalistic impressions of the company, the firm's competitiveness was eroding. Niche players, exciting new retail brands, were attacking M&S core and peripheral customers, and many in Britain simply viewed the firm as a relic institution. Mr. James Benfield was an M&S careerist. How can the firm be repositioned? How can M&S use its core competencies that worked so well at home in new and emerging markets?

Endnotes

1. Dow Jones Industrial, "Executive Report Marks & Spencer PLC," http://mrstg1s.djnr.com/cgi-bin/DJIntera..._binding=& get_name=null&searchText=U.MAR (accessed on May 26, 1999).

2. Sarah Marie De Nardi-Cole, "Marks and Spencer," in *International Retailing* (New York: Fairchild Publications, 1998): 159–166.

3. Ibid.

4. "Poor Marks," *The Economist*, November 21, 1998, 68.

5. "Angst in Their Pants," *Financial Times Weekend FT* 37 (June 1999): 7–10.

6. "Textiles: Unraveling," *The Economist*, January 2, 1999, 57–58.

7. Ibid.

8. "Angst in Their Pants," *Financial Times Weekend FT* 37 (June 1999): 10.

9. Sarah Marie De Nardi-Cole, "Marks and Spencer," in *International Retailing* (New York: Fairchild Publications, 1998): 159–166.

10. Ibid.

11. M&S (Marks & Spencer) 1999 Press Releases, www.marks-and-spencer.co.uk/corporate/press-releases/19990518.002.html (accessed on May 27, 1999).

12. Julia Flynn, "Marks & Sparks Isn't Throwing Off Any," *Business Week*, November 16, 1998, 64.

13. "Dress Sense," *The Economist*, May 22, 1999, 7.

14. "Angst in Their Pants," *Financial Times Weekend FT* 37 (June 1999): 7–10.

15. Dow Jones Industrial, "Executive Report Marks & Spencer PLC," http://mrstg1s.djnr.com/cgi-bin/DJIntera..._binding=&get_name=null&searchText=U.MAR (accessed on May 26, 1999).

16. "Angst in Their Pants," *Financial Times Weekend FT* 37 (June 1999): 7–10.

17. M&S (Marks & Spencer) 1999 Press Releases, www.marks-and-spencer.co.uk/corporate/press-releases/19990518.002.html (accessed on May 27, 1999).

18. Compiled by the author from 1999 Dow Jones Industrial and Market Guide data.

19. Julia Flynn, "Marks & Sparks Isn't Throwing Off Any," *Business Week*, November 16, 1998, 64.

20. "Angst in Their Pants," *Financial Times Weekend FT* 37 (June 1999): 7–10.

21. Ibid.

22. M&S (Marks & Spencer) 1999 Press Releases, www.marks-and-spencer.co.uk/corporate/press-releases/19990518.002.html (accessed on May 27, 1999).

23. "Angst in Their Pants," *Financial Times Weekend FT* 37 (June 1999): 7–10.

24. Lisa Campbell, "M&S Doubles Ad Budget in £20m Branding Review," *Marketing*, March 25, 1999, 9.

25. Sarah Marie De Nardi-Cole, "Marks and Spencer," in *International Retailing* (New York: Fairchild Publications, 1998): 159–166.

26. M&S (Marks & Spencer) 1999 Press Releases, www.marks-and-spencer.co.uk/corporate/press-releases/19990518.002.html (accessed on May 27, 1999).

27. Ibid.

28. "Angst in Their Pants," *Financial Times Weekend FT* 37 (June 1999): 7–10.

29. Sarah Marie De Nardi-Cole, "Marks and Spencer," in *International Retailing* (New York: Fairchild Publications, 1998): 159–166.

30. M&S 1998 Annual Report, www.marks-and-spencer.co.uk...ate/annual-report/Europe(Far-East or America)/main.html (accessed on October 9, 1998).

31. Ibid., p. 1.

32. "Angst in Their Pants," *Financial Times Weekend FT* 37 (June 1999): 7–10.

33. Sarah Marie De Nardi-Cole, "Marks and Spencer," in *International Retailing* (New York: Fairchild Publications, 1998): 159–166.

34. Ibid.

35. Alexandra Jardin, "Time for M&S to Follow Tesco," *Marketing*, January 28, 1999, 17–21.

36. Alexandra Jardin, "St. Michael's Evangelist," *Marketing*, April 22, 1999, 25–28.

37. Lisa Campbell, "M&S Doubles Ad Budget in Pounds 20m Branding Review," *Marketing*, March 25, 1999, 9.

38. A. Briggs, "St. Michael Marks and Spencer PLC," in *International Directory of Company Histories* (St. James: St. James Press, 1992): 124–126.

39. Sarah Marie De Nardi-Cole, "Marks and Spencer," in *International Retailing* (New York: Fairchild Publications, 1998): 159–166.

40. Maureen Whitehead, "International Franchising—Marks & Spencer: A Case Study," *International Journal of Retail & Distribution Management* 19, no. 2 (1991): 10–12.

41. Sarah Marie De Nardi-Cole, "Marks and Spencer," in *International Retailing* (New York: Fairchild Publications, 1998): 159–166.

42. Ilan Alon, "International Franchising Modes of Entry," in *Franchising Beyond the Millennium: Learning Lessons From the Past* (Society of Franchising 13th Annual Conference, 1999): Faye S. McIntyre and Sandra M. Huszagh, "Internationalization of Franchising Systems," *Journal of International Marketing* 3, no. 4 (1995): 39–56.

43. M&S 1998 Annual Report, www.marks-and-spencer.co.uk... ate/annual-report/Europe(Far-East   or   America)/main.html (accessed on October 9, 1998).

44. Sarah Marie De Nardi-Cole, "Marks and Spencer," in *International Retailing* (New York: Fairchild Publications, 1998): 159–166.

45. Ibid.

46. M&S 1998 Annual Report, www.marks-and-spencer.co.uk... ate/annual-report/Europe(Far-East   or   America)/main.html (accessed on October 9, 1998).

47. Maureen Whitehead, "International Franchising—Marks & Spencer: A Case Study," *International Journal of Retail & Distribution Management* 19, no. 2 (1991): 10–12.

48. Sarah Marie De Nardi-Cole, "Marks and Spencer," in *International Retailing* (New York: Fairchild Publications, 1998): 159–166.

49. Dow Jones Industrial, "Executive Report Marks & Spencer PLC," http://mrstg1s.djnr.com/cgi-bin/DJIntera..._binding= &get_name=null&searchText=U.MAR (accessed May 26, 1999).

50. M&S (Marks & Spencer) 1999 Press Releases, www.marks-and-spencer.co.uk/corporate/press-releases/19990518.002. html (accessed on May 27, 1999).

51. Sarah Marie De Nardi-Cole, "Marks and Spencer," in *International Retailing* (New York: Fairchild Publications, 1998): 159–166.

52. M&S 1998 Annual Report, www.marks-and-spencer.co.uk... ate/annual-report/Europe(Far-East or America)/main.html (accessed on October 9, 1998).

53. Sarah Marie De Nardi-Cole, "Marks and Spencer," in *International Retailing* (New York: Fairchild Publications, 1998): 159–166.

54. Julia Flynn, "Marks & Sparks Isn't Throwing Off Any," *Business Week*, November 16, 1998, 64.

55. J. Glew, "Meeting the European Challenge (Marks & Spencer)," *European Superstore Decisions* (Spring 1994): 46–49.

56. M&S (Marks & Spencer) 1999 Press Releases, www.marks-and-spencer.co.uk/corporate/press-releases/19990518.002. html (accessed on May 27, 1999).

57. M&S 1998 Annual Report, www.marks-and-spencer.co.uk... ate/annual-report/Europe(Far-East or America)/main.html (accessed on October 9, 1998).

58. Sarah Marie De Nardi-Cole, "Marks and Spencer," in *International Retailing* (New York: Fairchild Publications, 1998): 159–166.

59. Julia Flynn, "Marks & Sparks Isn't Throwing Off Any," *Business Week*, November 16, 1998, 64.

60. "Poor Marks," *The Economist*, November 21, 1998, 68.

61. "Textiles: Unraveling," *The Economist*, January 2, 1999, 57–58.

62. Julia Flynn, "Marks & Sparks Isn't Throwing Off Any," *Business Week*, November 16, 1998, 64.

63. "Poor Marks," *The Economist*, November 21, 1998, 68.

64. Matthew Gwyther, "King Richard: A Tragedy in Three Acts," *Management Today* (April 1999): 78–85.

65. Alexandra Jardin, "Time for M&S to Follow Tesco," *Marketing*, January 28, 1999, 17–21.

66. Philip Buxton, "M&S Chief Rejigs Retail Operation," *Marketing Week* 22, no. 12 (1999): 6.

67. George Pitcher, "Reality Forces UK Retail Giants to Check Out Their Strategic Options," *Marketing Week*, January 21, 1999, 21–24.

68. S. Eroglu, "The Internationalization Process of Franchise Systems: A Conceptual Model," *International Marketing Review* 9, no. 5 (1992): 19–30.

69. "Angst in Their Pants," *Financial Times Weekend FT* 37 (June 1999): 7–10.

70. Ibid.

71. Ibid.

Part II

In Search of Global Opportunities

5

Estimating Demand in Emerging Markets for Kodak Express

David M. Currie, Ilan Alon

Anna Johnson, a market analyst at Kodak, gazed at the information she had accumulated on various countries and wondered how she could use it to estimate the demand for Kodak Express (KE) outlets. She had learned from the Kodak market research department that demand for KE outlets depended on household income. To support one Kodak Express outlet, one of the following was needed: one million households with annual incomes equal to or exceeding the equivalent of US$15,000, two million households earning the equivalent of between US$10,000 and US$14,999, four million households earning the equivalent of between US$5,000 and US$9,999, or ten million households with incomes less than the equivalent of US$5,000 (see Table 5.1). According to the market research department, these averages seemed to apply throughout the world, when international dollars (purchasing power parity adjusted) were used as a benchmark.

Table 5.1 Number of Households and Income Levels Needed to Support One Kodak Express Outlet

Income	# of Households
≥$15,000	1 million
$10,000–$14,999	2 million
$5,000–$9,999	4 million
$0–$4,999	10 million

Source: Kodak company estimates/assumptions.

Unfortunately, the statistics Johnson was able to find did not tell her the household income in U.S. dollar equivalents in various countries or how many households in each country fell into a specific income bracket. She would need to complete a series of intermediate calculations to transform the original macroeconomic data to information that was useful for estimating the demand for Kodak Express outlets. Then, on the basis of market demand, Kodak would be able to use this information to decide how to allocate its investments across the various emerging markets.

The purpose of Johnson's calculations was to identify the markets with the most potential. The commitment to open KE outlets in a particular country was a significant investment that needed to have a promising return. Further, determining the markets with the most potential was in line with Kodak's philosophy of "investing where you sell the most."

Johnson sat in front of her computer, attempting to develop a model that would help her to estimate the market demand for KE outlets. She picked up a pencil and paper and began to sketch the process she would follow to use the data at her disposal to determine demand for KE outlets. Once she determined the process, she would prepare a spreadsheet model, plug in the data for a country, and see whether the result was reasonable.

Kodak's Global Strategy

The manufacture and distribution of photography items had been the major focus of Eastman Kodak Corporation since George Eastman commercialized personal cameras using roll film in 1888.[1] The next year, the company became international when it extended distribution of products outside the United States. In 1900, Kodak introduced the first Brownie camera, the company's effort to make photography available to a mass market. By 2002, the company's products were available in more than 150 countries. However, the company was faced with increased competition from two fronts: Japan's Fuji Photo Film Co. produced and marketed many of the same photography products as Kodak, and Kodak had been slow to respond to the emergence of digital photography.[2]

Worldwide revenues for Kodak's products exceeded US$5.5 billion in 2010, a decrease of US$800 million compared with 2009 and a decrease of US$1.6 billion compared with 2008. The decline was partially due to the global economic slowdown, particularly in Europe, the Middle East, and Africa: Revenues from these regions had decreased by more than US$1 billion in the previous two years.[3]

To offset the decline in sales volume in Europe, the Middle East, and Africa, Kodak's strategy was to expand sales into emerging markets such as India and China. Because of China's enormous population and its citizens' cultural affinity for taking pictures, China was one of the cornerstones of Kodak's emerging market strategy. Even expanding the market to just half of China's population would add the equivalent of another United States or Japan to the world photographic market.[4]

Kodak Express Outlets

Despite Kodak Express outlets being independently owned, they were contractually obliged to buy and display exclusively Kodak products, and they utilized Kodak's store specifications and the company's brand elements. The outlets provided three benefits to Kodak:

- A frontline retailing presence
- Wide distribution of Kodak products, services, and brand name
- A strategic asset for Kodak for market development

The company was making an effort to have a more extensive distribution of its Kodak Express outlets throughout the world. Through these outlets, Kodak planned to launch "grass-root marketing development programs."[5]

Data Availability

Johnson focused on four sets of data that were readily available from reliable sources for a variety of countries: population, purchasing power, income distribution, and average household size. The first data set, population, seemed straightforward. Any analysis of a country's purchasing habits would begin with consumers, whether on an individual (per capita) basis or a household basis. Population estimates for 2010 are shown in Table 5.2. More recent statistics were difficult to locate because most countries conducted a census only once every 10 years. Between censuses, all population statistics were estimates.

Table 5.2 Population of Selected Countries, 2010

Country	Population (in Millions)
United States	310
Bangladesh	164
Brazil	193
Cambodia	14
China	1,341
India	1,216
Indonesia	234
Laos	6
Malaysia	28
Nigeria	156
Pakistan	167
Russia	140
South Africa	50
Thailand	64
Vietnam	88

Source: International Monetary Fund, 2010.

Determining the dollar-equivalent level of income from one country to another was a more challenging task. Many statistics comparing one country with another merely converted data into U.S. dollars using an average exchange rate for the year. Although this method was useful for some purposes, it was potentially misleading when used for consumption patterns because it ignored the cost of living from one country to another. For example, a family earning RMB65,000 in China earned the equivalent of approximately US$10,000 using an exchange rate conversion of RMB6.5 RMB per U.S. dollar.[6] But RMB65,000 in China purchased much more than US$10,000 purchased in the United States; thus, the family in China would be considered much better off by Chinese standards, and their consumption patterns might be closer to a family in the United States earning US$48,000.

To account for this difference, economists frequently standardized data for differences in purchasing power, called purchasing power parity (PPP). Johnson was able to find gross domestic product (GDP) per capita in U.S. dollars using PPP for the countries in which she was interested (see Table 5.3).

Table 5.3 Gross Domestic Product Purchasing Power Parity Per Capita for Selected Countries, 2010

Country	Gross Domestic Product Purchasing Power Parity per Capita (in US$)
United States	47,284
Bangladesh	1,572
Brazil	11,239
Cambodia	2,112
China	7,519
India	3,339
Indonesia	4,394
Laos	2,436
Malaysia	14,670
Nigeria	2,422
Pakistan	2,791

Country	Gross Domestic Product Purchasing Power Parity per Capita (in US$)
Russia	15,837
South Africa	10,498
Thailand	9,187
Vietnam	3,134

Source: International Monetary Fund, 2010.

A related problem was that GDP was not the same as national income, and Johnson needed to know a household's income. After some research, she discovered that because the difference usually was not significant, economists frequently used GDP as a proxy for national income. Therefore, the GDP per capita for these countries could serve as a substitute for income per capita. That meant that the average person in India earned the equivalent of US$3,339 annually on a PPP basis in 2010.

Income distribution was another important issue because if more people earned low incomes in a country, they wouldn't be able to support as many KE outlets. Johnson needed to determine how many households corresponded to different income levels for any country. Data on income distribution are shown in Table 5.4. For any country, population was divided into equal portions called quintiles (fifths), and each quintile showed the share of national income accruing to that quintile. For example, in India the bottom 20 percent of the population accounted for 8.1 percent of national income, and the top 20 percent of the population accounted for 45.3 percent of national income. Because each quintile represented 20 percent of the population, about 243 million people (20 percent of 1,216 million people) earned only 8.1 percent of the country's total income. At the other extreme, 243.2 million people earned 45.3 percent of the country's total income. If incomes were distributed evenly in a country, each quintile would account for 20 percent of the national income (see Table 5.4).

Table 5.4 Distribution of Income for Selected Countries—Various Dates (as a Percentage of Income)

Quintile	United States	Bangladesh	Brazil	Cambodia	China	India	Indonesia	Laos
Upper	45.8	40.8	58.7	52	47.8	45.3	45.5	41.4
Upper Middle	22.4	21.1	19.6	18.9	22	20.4	21.3	21.6
Middle	15.7	16.1	11.8	12.9	14.7	14.9	14.9	16.2
Lower Middle	10.7	12.6	6.9	9.7	9.8	11.3	11	12.3
Lower	5.4	9.4	3	6.5	5.7	8.1	7.4	8.5

Quintile	Malaysia	Nigeria	Pakistan	Russia	South Africa	Thailand	Vietnam
Upper	44.4	48.6	40.5	50.2	62.7	49.4	45.4
Upper Middle	22.8	21.9	21.3	20.7	18.8	21.3	21.6
Middle	15.8	14.7	16.3	13.9	9.9	14.1	15.2
Lower Middle	10.8	9.7	12.8	9.6	5.6	9.4	10.8
Lower	6.4	5.1	9.1	5.6	3.1	5.9	7.1

Source: World Bank, World Development Indicators, various dates.

The average size of a household would help to determine the number of households in a country and, thus, the number of households in each of the quintiles. Data for the average size of household shown as the number of persons per household are shown in Table 5.5. Dividing the population of a quintile by the number of people per household would yield an estimate for the number of households in the country. Of course, the assumption was that the number of people per household did not change with income. Johnson realized, however, that average household size depended on both cultural and economic factors. In some countries, the custom was for an extended family (parents, children, and grandparents) to live in the same household. In most countries, household size varied according to the level of income in the household because families earning higher incomes tended to have fewer children. Household size also varied between urban and rural areas: Urban households tended to be smaller. For this analysis, Johnson would need to assume that the average household size applied throughout the country, simply because no reliable statistics were available on the differences between sizes of households for all the countries she wanted to examine.

Table 5.5 Average Household Size for Selected Countries, Various Dates

Country	Average Household Size (in Persons)
United States	2.6
Bangladesh	6.0
Brazil	3.6
Cambodia	3.2
China	3.4
India	5.3
Indonesia	3.4
Laos	5.2
Malaysia	4.4
Nigeria	4.9
Pakistan	7.2
Russia	2.7

Country	Average Household Size (in Persons)
South Africa	3.7
Thailand	3.5
Vietnam	4.4

Source: Euromonitor International, 2010.

Calculating Potential Demand

As Johnson thought more about her task, she realized that she faced a two-step problem. First, she would need to calculate the household income in U.S. dollars for each quintile of the population. Only by doing this step would she then be able to separate households into each of the income brackets. This difference was important because each category was able to support a different number of KE outlets, as Johnson had learned from Kodak's market research department. The second step would be to calculate the potential demand for KE outlets once she knew the number of households in each spending category.

To attain this number, Johnson knew that she would need to complete several interim steps. Using her available data, she could make some initial calculations: She could determine the PPP GDP for the entire population, the population per quintile, and the number of households per quintile. Using the population's GDP and each country's income distribution, she could then calculate the income per quintile.

Dividing the income per quintile by the population per quintile, she knew she would derive the individual income per quintile, from which she could easily conclude the household income per quintile. Then, using the household income per quintile, she would be able to determine how many households fell into each of the categories in Table 5.1. Knowing how many households fell in each category, she could then determine the potential demand for KE outlets in a specific market. Her goal was to build a model that would enable her to evaluate each of the countries in Table 5.2. She would test the model using the data for one country. If it worked, the computer would then do most or all of the subsequent calculations. Once the model was complete, Johnson would use it both to predict demand for Kodak Express outlets in selected emerging markets and to make recommendations to Kodak management regarding market entry and resource allocations in these countries.

Finally, Johnson knew that such a significant investment should take not only today's demand into account. To determine the most attractive markets, she would also need to determine whether those markets would still be attractive in the future. Therefore, she decided to also calculate, in addition to the 2010 calculations, each country's demand for the year 2016. She was able to gather projected data on both PPP GDP per capita and populations for 2016 (see Tables 5.6 and 5.7); however, she was unable to find reliable forecasts for income distribution and average household sizes. She therefore made the naive assumption that these last two variables, income distribution and average household size, would not change significantly.

Table 5.6 Forecasted Population for Selected Countries for 2016

Country	Population (in Millions)
United States	328
Bangladesh	178
Brazil	199
Cambodia	15
China	1,382
India	1,316
Indonesia	253
Laos	7
Malaysia	31
Nigeria	183
Pakistan	183

Country	Population (in Millions)
Russia	137
South Africa	53
Thailand	66
Vietnam	95

Source: International Monetary Fund, 2011.

Table 5.7 Forecasted Gross Domestic Product Purchasing Power Parity Per Capita for Selected Countries for 2016

Country	Gross Domestic Product Purchasing Power Parity Per Capita (in US $)
United States	57,320
Bangladesh	2,340
Brazil	15,193
Cambodia	3,183
China	13,729
India	5,398
Indonesia	6,556
Laos	3,675
Malaysia	19,541
Nigeria	3,242
Pakistan	3,678
Russia	22,717
South Africa	13,607
Thailand	12,681
Vietnam	4,803

Source: International Monetary Fund, 2011.

What is the potential demand for KE outlets in the various emerging markets in 2010? What would be the demand by 2016? Given the assumptions, which markets will be the top candidates for investment?

We wish to thank Christopher Gassner for the collection of data and the development of new spreadsheets.

Endnotes

1. Kodak, "Building the Foundation," http://kodak.com/US/en/corp/kodakHistory/buildingTheFoundation.shtml   (accessed January 26, 2004).

2. Daniel Gross, "Photo Finished: Why Eastman Kodak Deserves to Lose Its Dow Jones Industrial Average Membership," *Slate*, January 6, 2004, http://slate.msn.com/id/2093512/ (accessed January 26, 2004).

3. Kodak 2010 Annual Report, www.envisionreports.com/EK/2011/22103MA11E/38495aae46f94783a4829c3e66124a12/Kodak_AR_10k_Secured_3-28-11.pdf (accessed June 16, 2011).

4. David Swift, "Remarks of David Swift, Chairman & President, Greater China Region, Eastman Kodak Company" (Goldman Sachs 21st Century China Conference, September 1999, 1–8).

5. Ilan Alon, "Interview: International Franchising with Kodak in China," *Thunderbird International Business Review*, November/December 2001, 737–754.

6. Exchange rate on April 18, 2011, http://finance.yahoo.com/currency-converter/ (accessed June 16, 2011).

6

Ruth's Chris Steak House: The High Stakes of International Expansion

Allen H. Kupetz, Ilan Alon

"Well, I was so lucky that I fell into something that I really, really love. And I think that if you ever go into business, you better find something you really love, because you spend so many hours with it ... it almost becomes your life."

—Ruth Fertel, 1927–2002, Founder of Ruth's Chris Steak House

In 2006, Ruth's Chris Steak House (Ruth's Chris) was fresh off a sizzling initial public offering (IPO). Dan Hannah, vice president for business development since June 2004, was responsible for the development of a new business strategy focused on continued growth of franchise and company-operated restaurants. He also oversaw franchisee relations. Now a public company, Ruth's Chris had to meet Wall Street's expectations for revenue growth. Current stores were seeing consistent incremental revenue growth, but new restaurants were critical and Hannah knew that the international opportunities offered a tremendous upside.

With restaurants in just five countries including the United States, the challenge for Hannah was to decide where to go to next. Ruth's Chris regularly received inquiries from would-be franchisees all over the world, but strict criteria—liquid net worth of at least US$1 million, verifiable experience within the hospitality industry, and an ability and desire to develop multiple locations—eliminated many of the prospects. And the cost of a franchise—a US$100,000 per restaurant franchise fee, a five percent of gross sales royalty fee, and a two percent of gross sales fee as a contribution to the national advertising campaign—eliminated some qualified prospects. All this was coupled with a debate within Ruth's Chris senior management team about the need and desire to grow its international business. So where was Hannah to look for new international franchisees and what countries would be best suited for the fine dining that made Ruth's Chris famous?

The House That Ruth Built

Ruth Fertel, the founder of Ruth's Chris, was born in New Orleans in 1927. She skipped several grades in grammar school, and later entered Louisiana State University in Baton Rouge at the age of 15 to pursue degrees in chemistry and physics. After graduation, Fertel landed a job teaching at McNeese State University. The majority of her students were football players who not only towered over her, but were actually older than she was. Fertel taught for two semesters. In 1948, the former Ruth Ann Adstad married Rodney Fertel who lived in Baton Rouge and shared her love of horses. They had two sons, Jerry and Randy. They opened a racing stable in Baton Rouge. Ruth Fertel earned a thoroughbred trainer's license, making her the first female horse trainer in Louisiana. Ruth and Rodney Fertel divorced in 1958.

In 1965, Ruth Fertel spotted an ad in the *New Orleans Times-Picayune* selling a steak house. She mortgaged her home for US$22,000 to purchase Chris Steak House, a 60-seat restaurant on the corner of Broad and Ursuline in New Orleans, near the fairgrounds racetrack. In September of 1965, the city of New Orleans was ravaged by Hurricane Betsy just a few months after Fertel purchased Chris Steak House. The restaurant was left without power, so she cooked everything she had and brought it to her brother in devastated Plaquemines Parish to aid in the relief effort.

In 1976, the thriving restaurant was destroyed in a kitchen fire. Fertel bought a new property a few blocks away on Broad Street and soon opened under a new name, "Ruth's Chris Steak House," because her original contract with former owner, Chris Matulich, precluded her from using the name Chris Steak House in a different location. After years of failed attempts, Tom Moran, a regular customer and business owner from Baton Rouge, convinced a hesitant Fertel to let him open the first Ruth's Chris franchise in 1976. It opened on Airline Highway in Baton Rouge. Fertel reluctantly began awarding more and more franchises. In the 1980s, the little corner steak house grew into a global phenomenon with restaurants opening every year in cities around the nation and the world. Fertel became something of an icon herself and was dubbed by her peers *The First Lady of American Restaurants*.

Ruth's Chris grew to become the largest fine dining steak house in the United States (see Table 6.1) with its focus on an unwavering commitment to customer satisfaction and its broad selection of USDA Prime grade steaks (USDA Prime is a meat grade label that refers to evenly distributed marbling that enhances the flavor of the steak). The menu also included premium quality lamb chops, veal chops, fish, chicken, and lobster. Steak and seafood combinations and a vegetable platter were also available at selected restaurants. Dinner entrees were generally priced between US$18 to US$38. Three company-owned restaurants were open for lunch and offered entrees generally ranging in price from US$11 to US$24. The Ruth's Chris core menu was similar at all of its restaurants. The company occasionally introduced new items as specials that allowed the restaurant to offer its guests additional choices, such as items inspired by Ruth's Chris New Orleans heritage.[1]

Table 6.1 Fine Dining Steak Houses by Brand in the United States (2005)

Company Name	Number of Restaurants
Ruth's Chris	92
Morton's	66
Fleming's	32
Palm	28
Capital Grille	22
Shula's	16
Sullivan's	15
Smith & Wollensky	11
Del Frisco	6

Source: Ruth's Chris Steak House files.

In 2005, Ruth's Chris enjoyed a significant milestone, completing a successful IPO that raised more than US$154 million in new equity capital. In their 2005 Annual Report, the company said it had plans "to embark on an accelerated development plan and expand our footprint through both company-owned and franchised locations." 2005 restaurant sales grew to a record US$415.8 million from 82 locations in the United States and 10 international locations (see Figure 6.1) including Canada (1995, 2003), Hong Kong (1997, 2001), Mexico (1993, 1996, 2001), and Taiwan (1993, 1996, 2001). As of December 2005, 41 of the 92 Ruth's Chris restaurants were company-owned and 51 were franchisee-owned, including all 10 of the international restaurants (see Table 6.2).

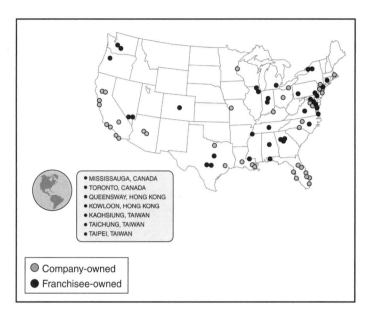

Figure 6.1 Ruth's Chris locations in the United States (2005)

Source: Ruth's Chris Steak House files.

Table 6.2 Ruth's Chris Restaurant Growth by Decade

Decade	New Restaurants (Total)	New Restaurants (Company-Owned)	New Restaurants (Franchises)
1965–1969	1	1	0
1970–1979	4	2	2
1980–1989	19	8	11
1990–1999	44	19	25
2000–2005	25	12	13
	93^2	42	51

Source: Ruth's Chris Steak House files.

Ruth's Chris's 51 franchisee-owned restaurants were owned by just 17 franchisees, with 5 new franchisees having the rights to develop a new restaurant, and the 3 largest franchisees owning 8, 6, and 5 restaurants, respectively. Prior to 2004, each franchisee entered into a 10-year franchise agreement with three 10-year renewal options for each restaurant. Each agreement granted the franchisee territorial protection, with the option to develop a certain number of restaurants in their territory. Ruth's Chris's franchisee agreements generally included termination clauses in the event of nonperformance by the franchisee.[3]

A World of Opportunities

As part of the international market selection process, Hannah considered four standard models (see Figure 6.2):

- **Product development**—New kinds of restaurants in existing markets
- **Diversification**—New kinds of restaurants in new markets
- **Penetration**—More of the same restaurants in the same market
- **Market development**—More of the same restaurants in new markets

Restaurant Brands

	Existing	New
Existing	**Penetration** (more restaurants) *Same market,* *Same product*	**Product Development** (new brands) *Same market,* *New product*
New	**Market Development** (new markets) *New market,* *Same product*	**Diversification** (new brands for new market) *New product,* *New market*

Market

Figure 6.2 Restaurant Growth Paths

Source: This diagram is based on Ansoff's Product/Market Matrix, first published in "Strategies for Diversification," *Harvard Business Review*, 1957.

The product development model (new kinds of restaurants in existing markets) was never seriously considered by Ruth's Chris. It had built a brand based on fine dining steak houses and, with only 92 stores, the company saw little need and no value in diversifying with new kinds of restaurants.

The diversification model (new kinds of restaurants in new markets) was also never considered by Ruth's Chris. In only four international markets, Hannah knew that the current fine dining steak house model would work in new markets without the risk of brand dilution or brand confusion.

The penetration model (more of the same restaurants in the same market) was already under way in a small way with new restaurants opening up in Canada. The limiting factor was simply that fine dining establishments would never be as ubiquitous as quick service restaurants (i.e., fast food) like McDonald's. Even the largest cities in the world would be unlikely to host more than five to six Ruth's Chris steak houses.

The market development model (more of the same restaurants in new markets) appeared the most obvious path to increased revenue. Franchisees in the four international markets—Canada, Hong Kong, Mexico, and Taiwan—were profitable and could offer testimony to would-be franchisees of the value of a Ruth's Chris franchise.

With the management team agreed on a model, the challenge shifted to market selection criteria. The key success factors were well-defined:

- **Beef-eaters**—Ruth's Chris was a steak house (though there were several fish items on the menu) and, thus, its primary customers were people who enjoy beef. According to the World Resources Institute, in 2002 there were 17 countries above the mean per capita of annual beef consumption for high-income countries (93.5 kilograms—see Table 6.3).[4]

- **Legal to import U.S. beef**—The current Ruth's Chris model used only USDA Prime beef, thus it had to be exportable to the target country. In some cases, Australian beef was able to meet the same high U.S. standard.

- **Population/high urbanization rates**—With the target customer being a well-to-do beef-eater, restaurants needed to be in densely populated areas to have a large enough pool. Most large centers probably met this requirement.

- **High disposable income**—Ruth's Chris is a fine dining experience and the average cost of a meal for a customer ordering an entrée was over US$70 at a Ruth's Chris in the United States. Although this might seem to eliminate many countries quickly, there are countries (e.g., China) that have such large populations that even a very small percentage of high disposable income people could create an appropriate pool of potential customers.

- **Do people go out to eat?**—This was a critical factor. If well-to-do beef-eaters did not go out to eat, these countries had to be removed from the target list.

- **Affinity for U.S. brands**—The name "Ruth's Chris" was uniquely American as was the Ruth Fertel story. Countries that were overtly anti-United States would be eliminated from—or at least pushed down—the target list. One measure of affinity could be the presence of existing U.S. restaurants and successful franchises.

Table 6.3 Meat Consumption Per Capita (in Kilograms)

Region/ Classification	2002	2001	2000	1999	1998	Growth Rate 1998–2002
World	39.7	38.8	38.6	38.0	37.7	5.31%
Asia (excluding Middle East)	27.8	26.9	26.6	25.7	25.4	9.45%

Region/ Classification	2002	2001	2000	1999	1998	Growth Rate 1998–2002
Central America/ Caribbean	46.9	45.7	44.8	42.9	41.3	13.56%
Europe	74.3	72.5	70.5	70.6	73.1	1.64%
Middle East/ North Africa	25.7	25.7	26.0	25.1	24.7	4.05%
North America	123.2	119.1	120.5	122.2	118.3	4.14%
South America	69.7	68.4	69.1	67.6	64.2	8.57%
Sub-Saharan Africa	13.0	12.9	13.1	12.8	12.6	3.17%
Developed countries	80.0	78.0	77.2	77.3	77.6	3.09%
Developing countries	28.9	28.1	28.0	27.1	26.6	8.65%
High-income countries	93.5	91.9	92.0	92.2	90.9	2.86%
Low-income countries	8.8	8.6	8.4	8.3	8.2	7.32%
Middle-income countries	46.1	44.6	43.9	42.7	42.3	8.98%

Source: World Resources Institute, "Meat Consumption: Per Capita (1984–2002)," http://earthtrends.wri.org/text/agriculture-food/variable-193.html (accessed June 7, 2006).

What Should Ruth's Chris Do Next?

Hannah had many years of experience in the restaurant franchising business, and thus had both personal preferences and good instincts about where Ruth's Chris should be looking for new markets. "Which markets should we enter first?" he thought to himself. Market entry was critical, but there were other issues too. Should franchising continue to be Ruth's Chris exclusive international mode of entry? Were there opportunities for joint ventures or company-owned stores in certain markets? How could he identify and evaluate new potential franchisees? Was there an opportunity to find a global partner/brand with which to partner?

Hannah gathered information from several reliable U.S. government and related Web sites and created the table in Table 6.4. He noted that many of his top prospects currently did not allow the importation of U.S. beef, but he felt that this was a political (rather than a cultural) variable and thus could change quickly under the right circumstances and with what he felt was the trend toward ever-more free trade. He could not find any data on how often people went out to eat or a measure of their affinity toward U.S. brands. Maybe the success of U.S. casual dining restaurants in a country might be a good indicator of how its citizens felt toward U.S. restaurants. With his spreadsheet open, he went to work on the numbers and began contemplating the future global expansion of the company.

Table 6.4 Data Table

Country	Per Capita Beef Consumption (kg)	Population (1,000s)	Urbanization Rate (%)	Per Capita GDP (PPP in US$)
Argentina	97.6	39,921	90%	$13,100
Bahamas	123.6	303	89%	$20,200
Belgium	86.1	10,379	97%	$31,400
Brazil	82.4	188,078	83%	$8,400
Chile	66.4	16,134	87%	$11,300
China	52.4	1,313,973	39%	$6,800
Costa Rica	40.4	4,075	61%	$11,100
Czech Rep	77.3	10,235	74%	$19,500
France	101.1	60,876	76%	$29,900
Germany	82.1	82,422	88%	$30,400
Greece	78.7	10,688	61%	$22,200
Hungary	100.7	9,981	65%	$16,300
Ireland	106.3	4,062	60%	$41,000
Israel	97.1	6,352	92%	$24,600
Italy	90.4	58,133	67%	$29,200
Japan	43.9	127,463	65%	$31,500

Country	Per Capita Beef Consumption (kg)	Population (1,000s)	Urbanization Rate (%)	Per Capita GDP (PPP in US$)
Kuwait	60.2	2,418	96%	$19,200
Malaysia	50.9	24,385	64%	$12,100
Netherlands	89.3	16,491	66%	$30,500
Panama	54.5	3,191	57%	$7,200
Poland	78.1	38,536	62%	$13,300
Portugal	91.1	10,605	55%	$19,300
Russia	51	142,893	73%	$11,100
Singapore	71.1	4,492	100%	$28,100
South Africa	39	44,187	57%	$12,000
South Korea	48	48,846	80%	$20,400
Spain	118.6	40,397	77%	$25,500
Switzerland	72.9	7,523	68%	$32,300
Turkey	19.3	70,413	66%	$8,200
UAE/Dubai	74.4	2,602	85%	$43,400
U.K.	79.6	60,609	89%	$30,300
United States	124.8	298,444	80%	$41,800
Vietnam	28.6	84,402	26%	$2,800

Source: World Resources Institute, "Meat Consumption: Per Capita (1984–2002)," http://earth-trends.wri.org/text/agriculture-food/variable-193.html (accessed June 7, 2006) and World Bank Key Development Data & Statistics, http://web.worldbank.org/WBSITE/EXTERNAL/DATASTATI STICS/0,,contentMDK:20535285~menuPK:232599~pagePK:64133150~piPK:64133175~theSit ePK:239419,00.html (accessed June 7, 2006).

Endnotes

1. Ruth's Chris Steak House 2005 Annual Report, p. 7.
2. Due to damage caused by Hurricane Katrina, Ruth's Chris was forced to temporarily close its restaurant in New Orleans, Louisiana.

3. Ruth's Chris Steak House 2005 Annual Report, p. 10.

4. World Resources Institute, "Meat Consumption: Per Capita (1984–2002)," http://earthtrends.wri.org/text/agriculture-food/variable-193.html (accessed June 7, 2006).

Part III

Franchising in Emerging Markets and Developing Countries

7

Master International Franchising in China: The Athlete's Foot, Inc. (Part A)

Amber Xu, Ilan Alon

One day in late 2001, Rick Wang, the managing director of RetailCo, Inc., the master franchisee for The Athlete's Foot in China, was reviewing the most recent sales report of his company. He found that the sales volume for the past six months had declined precipitously, down almost one-third from what it had been only one year ago. Inevitably, Wang was concerned.

RetailCo, Inc. had enjoyed a banner year in 2000; however, the company had experienced a cascade of problems beginning in 2001. At the start of that year, the company was forced to deal with pressure due to a supply shortage of major products, which could deal a deathblow to any small retailer. In quick succession, financial crises and sales problems related to the lack of product created a systemic disaster. Unless Wang acted quickly and decisively, RetailCo might not survive this confluence of major problems.

Rick Wang and RetailCo, Inc.

Rick Wang was a typical American-born Chinese, able to speak both American English and Chinese. His parents had immigrated to Taiwan and then America when they were fairly young; regardless of their geographic location, however, the family maintained strong cultural ties to its homeland. Wang was raised in a traditional Chinese family in the United States. After graduating from the University of

Southern California with a degree in communications, he began his career as an account director at Lintas, a well-regarded international advertising agency. He then transferred to Foremost Dairies Ltd., a leading manufacturer of milk and ice cream in Taiwan, as its marketing director, and thus gained experience in short-shelf-life consumer goods.

In 1992, he moved to his parents' hometown, Shanghai, and worked for Shanghai Fuller Foods Ltd. as vice president of marketing. He assisted in the building of the company's factory in the Jinqiao district and developed new brands of Fuller milk and ice cream. Under Wang's leadership, the brands "Qian Shi Nai" (milk) and "San Marlo" (ice cream) quickly achieved market leadership in the area, known by almost all the residents in Shanghai. In late 1997, Shanghai Fuller Foods Ltd. was sold to Nestlé; Wang decided to strike out on his own.

As a result of a chance encounter, Rick Wang became acquainted with the athletic footwear industry and became a retailer. Wang retains a vivid memory of the day he was introduced to the possibilities of this retailing niche:

> One day, when I was playing softball with a bunch of my American friends who then worked at Nike, one of them said to me, "Rick, since your ice-cream business has been sold, what do you want to do now?" I said, "I don't know yet. Maybe I'll go back to San Francisco, or back to Taiwan." He said, "Why don't you consider overseeing our Nike stores in Shanghai?" I asked, "Nike stores? Can I make money?" And he replied immediately, "Sure, they can make a lot of money!" I asked for the financial statement, which he showed me the next day. After looking carefully I said, "OK. Let's do it."

Rick Wang, at that time, had no experience in either the sports footwear industry or any direct knowledge of in-store retailing, but he was very excited about his new business venture. RetailCo, Inc., was established with the intention of managing the retail realities of athletic footwear sales.

His optimism notwithstanding, Wang's hasty involvement and lack of experience in the footwear retailing industry led to the poor performance of his stores. In the six months after the company was established, no profit was made. As the situation worsened, Wang anxiously sought expert advice. He began by educating himself on the Internet, searching terms such as "athletic footwear retail," "sport retail," and "sports shoes retail"; surprisingly, he found that almost every page of his searches revealed one American company: The Athlete's Foot, Inc. Like many entrepreneurs, Wang recognized the value inherent in modeling his own activities on those of an industry leader.

The Athlete's Foot, Inc.

The Athlete's Foot, Inc., based in Kennesaw, Georgia, in the United States, was the world's foremost franchisor of athletic-footwear operations. It grew from a small, family-run store to an international retailer in three decades. The Athlete's Foot owned about 800 corporate and franchise stores in more than 40 countries (see Table 7.1).

Table 7.1 Countries Where The Athlete's Foot Stores Are Located

Antigua	China	Greece	Kuwait	Poland
Argentina	Costa Rica	Guadeloupe	Malaysia	Portugal
Aruba	Curacao	Guatemala	Malta	Republic of Palau
Australia	Cyprus	Hungary	Martinique	Reunion Island
Bahamas	Denmark	Indonesia	Mexico	St. Kitts/ St. Nevis
Barbados	Dominican Republic	Italy	New Zealand	St. Maarten
Canada	Ecuador	Jamaica	Panama	South Korea
Cayman Islands	France	Japan	Peru	United States
Chile	French Guyana	Jersey Island	Philippines	Venezuela

Source: www.theathletesfoot.com

The history of the growth of The Athlete's Foot was a model of aggressive business behavior. In 1971, Robert and David Lando opened the world's first athletic-footwear specialty store, named The Athlete's Foot, on Wood Street in Pittsburgh, Pennsylvania. The very next year, The Athlete's Foot, Inc., began franchising its business model domestically. The first franchise agreement was signed by Killian Spanbauer, who opened a store at the Sawyer Street Shopping Center in Oshkosh, Wisconsin. After that, The Athlete's Foot began a period of focused expansion: By 1976, there were more than 100 stores; only two years later (1978), there were more than 200 Athlete's Foot outlets in America.

That same year, the company began to internationalize its franchising efforts; in 1978, the first of what was to become many international franchises opened, at 16 Stevens Place, in Adelaide, Australia. This milestone event encouraged The Athlete's Foot to franchise an additional 150 stores in international markets by 1979.

After a decade of successful market penetration, The Athlete's Foot, in its second decade, began a period of adjustment. In the early 1980s, Group Rallye purchased The Athlete's Foot from the Lando family. This buyout provided crucial financial support to the company at a time when it needed to pay more attention to product design and customer service, rather than focusing exclusively on expansion. For example, the company inaugurated a systemwide commitment to customer service. In order to help customers find the "right" footwear, or at least to help determine the proper fit, sales associates underwent training at "Fit University," introduced by The Athlete's Foot Wear Test Center to provide education on the physiology and anatomy of the feet and to enable sales associates to properly fit athletic footwear. This focus on educating its sales force—who, in turn, educated customers about the value of relying on The Athlete's Foot as a consumer-oriented facility—paid almost immediate dividends.

In the 1990s, The Athlete's Foot consolidated its market standing even as it continued its enviable international growth. The Athlete's

Foot changed its name to The Athlete's Foot, Inc., and moved its headquarters to Kennesaw, Georgia, after Euris purchased Group Rallye in 1991. The company's structure was reorganized into two divisions as a result of this change in ownership: A marketing team serviced the franchises, and a "store team" operated the company-owned stores. The marketing team did an impressive job in the years following the reorganization. The Athlete's Foot, Inc., grew to more than 650 stores worldwide in 1997 and was named the number-one franchise opportunity by *Success* magazine that same year. After a dynamic new chief executive officer (CEO), Robert J. Corliss, joined the company in 1999, the company experienced a record growth year—opening 37 corporate stores in six countries and 87 franchise stores, the most franchises in company history. The other division, the operations' team that managed company stores, also achieved significant success during this period. The company launched a new store design featuring an innovative, customer-oriented technology called the FitPrint System.[1] This innovation was to lead to a competitive advantage for The Athlete's Foot, Inc. As a result of franchise oversight and marketing innovations, the company was awarded the "Trendsetter of the Year" award by the sporting goods community for 1999 and 2000.

The growth story of The Athlete's Foot became a model for franchising even as it successfully continued its almost 30-year tradition of domestic and international expansion. Many would-be entrepreneurs were drawn to the company, for reasons linked to the company's focus points: customer service, aggressive marketing, and control of the pipeline from production to point of sale. Comments from franchisees illustrate the company's magnetic effect on franchisee development. Jaclyn Hill from Auburn said that her "decision to join The Athlete's Foot was based primarily upon them having an established, customer-service focused program to sell athletic shoes." Powell's Kyle H. Johnson commented:

The Athlete's Foot was my choice when I decided to enter the retail industry for several reasons. Some are obvious such as access to vendors, reasonable franchise fees, and fair royalty rates. Beyond that, they offer a tremendous amount of support.[2]

The Athlete's Foot Master Franchisee in China

Rick Wang was one of many entrepreneurs interested in pursuing business opportunities in the footwear retailing sector; Wang, however, had not followed the less-risky entrepreneurial path of franchising, but had struck out on his own, with problematic results. His research on the successes of The Athlete's Foot's management model led him to contact that company. At that time, Wang had little knowledge of how franchising worked, or what potential benefits he might realize. In fact, his ostensible reason for contacting the company was his belief that he might pick up some pointers from this more experienced retailer:

> I was not a believer in franchising. I did not believe in franchising because I did not believe in paying so much money to buy somebody's brand and then putting more money in to build it. I can do [that] by myself. But I decided to contact The Athlete's Foot because I really knew that I needed help.

Rick Wang decided to fly to Atlanta, to view the company's headquarters and evaluate the company and its team. This trip was fruitful. As a potential Chinese partner, Wang received a warm welcome from the CEO and the entire management team during his visit. Among his stops, he was especially impressed by the inventory-control system in the merchandize department. Wang recalled:

> I wasn't very excited until I walked into the merchandize department and I saw their buying team, how they bought products. I saw how intensively they controlled the inventory

system, using a very high-tech system. And then I started to learn the science behind the retailing. And I started to realize perhaps I need to pay the tuition to learn this. It's always the case: If you want to dance, you have to pay the band.

After Wang returned to China, he immediately started his franchise and retail plan. He first persuaded the board of RetailCo to agree to his idea of becoming the master franchisee of The Athlete's Foot structure in China. Second, he efficiently worked out a negotiations' plan with the U.S. franchisor on the subjects of sales territory and royalty fees. He suggested separating the huge Chinese market into three regions: East China Area, North China Area, and South China Area. The region of East China, stretching to the cities of Chengdu and Chongqin, was the biggest and potentially the most important market in China; it was in this area that Wang planned to focus his efforts. The region of North China, including Beijing, although a potentially lucrative market, was to be a secondary consideration. Last, development of the South China Area was to be delayed until after the first two regions were penetrated; the proximity to Hong Kong, with its history of appropriating brand names and flooding the market with cheaper copies, made immediate consideration of this region a risky and ambiguous proposition.

In terms of royalty fees, Wang fortunately negotiated a fairly good deal with The Athlete's Foot, Inc. The monthly royalty was to be 2.5% of net sales. Other initial-area development fees—including franchising fees, fees for additional stores, purchasing a management information system (MIS), an employment-control system, etc.—totaled a few thousand dollars per store. In addition, Wang requested discounts related to any future fees for local marketing. All the funds for initiating business were to be self-financed.

When the deal was made, Wang, together with his six colleagues, went to Atlanta for "New Owner Training" at The Athlete's Foot's, Inc. Within six weeks, they had completed their "On Site Training" and had practiced operating the business: They worked in a store, sold shoes, helped people with their fittings, and even worked in the warehouse, experiencing firsthand the realities of inventory control. They also learned how to work internal-control systems and marketing procedures. Overall, their training covered issues related to marketing, merchandizing, operations' management, and employee sales training. Wang commented: "It was just fascinating, like going back to school. It was very enjoyable."

Their efforts paid off. In September 1998, the first store of the nascent master franchisee's China operation was opened in the Parkson Department Store on the Huaihai Road in Shanghai, in the East China Area. Parkson was the most popular department store with an ideal demographic: The youngest customers between the age of 20 to 35—those considered most devoted to brand names and most style conscious—shopped on fashion-oriented Huaihai Road. Therefore, the first store was actually in the fashion center amid a favorite venue of young consumers. The store was opened on the ground floor of Parkson's with the same store design and equipment as those in the United States. Beautiful store design and abundant/diverse name-brand products made the store attractive to customers.

Wang achieved success in starting his retail franchising at a time when the franchise concept in the Chinese market was new and innovative, and the sports footwear market was underdeveloped. His business instincts, his knowledge of the Shanghai market, and his training at The Athlete's Foot, Inc.'s headquarters combined to initiate a signal success in what was then a relatively new entrepreneurial concept.

Business Context

The Chinese franchising market was different from that of the United States. Franchising was much less developed in China and its penetration in retail and service sales and in the overall economy was relatively negligible, albeit with a high potential for future growth. RetailCo and Athlete's Foot wanted to capitalize on this future prospect growth and pent-up demand for athletic branded shoes in China.

Franchising in the Chinese Market

The franchise concept first entered the Chinese market in the early years of the 1990s with the emergence of reputable international franchising companies, such as KFC and McDonald's. They originally entered China in the early 1990s, building corporate stores first. After having achieved steady sales volumes and sufficient economies of scale, they cautiously but aggressively expanded. These pioneer global franchisors included dominant players in the fast-food industry and various master franchisors in other industries, such as 7-Eleven convenience stores, 21st Century Real Estate, EF education, Avis auto rental, Kodak film developing, and Fornet laundry service. These firms contributed to China's franchising market development and created an awareness among an increasingly entrepreneurial class that franchising held substantial positive outcomes for those able to enter into such relationships.

Overseas franchisors tended to adopt one of two approaches when operating in the Chinese market: the franchise of a product or trade name (product name franchising) or the franchise of a particular business model in exchange for fees or royalties (business format franchising). Corporations that had a strong capital background, such as McDonald's and KFC, would choose an offshore franchise retail model (see Figure 7.1) to ensure effective control over product quality and company operations. Small- and medium-sized franchisors would often choose direct franchising by seeking a local franchisee (see Figure 7.2). Franchisors, licensing to local partners, could take advantage of local knowledge, saving the costs resulting from distance—both in terms of logistics and culture.

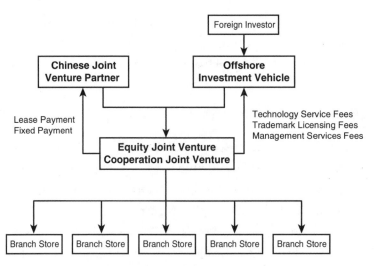

Figure 7.1 Offshore franchise retail model

Source: Fraser Medel, "Legal Issues Related to Franchising in China," *Franchising in China*, November 2003.

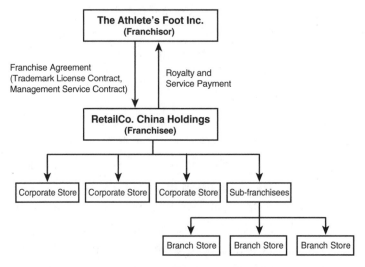

Figure 7.2 Franchise structures of The Athlete's Foot in China

Since the end of the 1990s, franchising had become a mature, steady growth opportunity in China. By the end of 1997, there were just more than 90 franchisors in China and about 30 franchise stores. One year later, however, the number had grown to more than 120 franchisors with sales volume of more than 50 million RMB (US$6.05

million), of which 40% were franchise stores.[3] By 2000, the number of franchisors approached 600. The sales volume also increased dramatically, jumping about 80% from 1999 to 2000.[4] This remarkable growth (at the time of this article, franchising was growing at a high double-digit growth rate) continued in the years that followed.

Franchised businesses in China varied along a wide spectrum of business sectors. Companies in more than 30 industries had chosen franchising as a business model to sell their products and expand in this market. Retail and food/restaurant operations had always been the dominant franchising industries, accounting for 35% and 30% of total franchisors,[5] respectively. Other segments experiencing significant growth included education, business services, auto services, interior decoration, beauty and health, and laundry. The service sector had also grown in importance in recent years.

Market Environment

In the late 1990s, as many in the global market were aware, China was becoming the land of opportunity. China's strong and steady growth, proven by 10 years of continual gross domestic product (GDP) increases, seemed unstoppable. Economic growth led to an increase in personal incomes, especially in larger cities. The emergence of a large middle class, often consisting of well-educated professionals, added to the consumer demand for globally recognized, quality products.

Domestically, the Chinese government made great efforts to regulate the market and standardize the business environment. To facilitate access to the World Trade Organization (WTO), China committed itself to removing more market-entry barriers, which created a more open market for international investors. The laws and regulations governing franchise businesses were, thus, improved. On November 14, 1997, the Ministry of Internal Trade published and released the very first Chinese franchise law, *The Regulation on Commercial Franchise*

Business (for Trial Implementation). Afterward, the Regulation was revised and improved several times: In 2005, *The Law on Commercial Franchise Business Administration* was eventually released as a basic rule for franchise operations in China.

Market competition in China was less rigorous than that in the United States. In the athletic footwear retailing industry in China, for example, there were few capable players in the early to mid-1990s. Meanwhile, the demand for high-quality athletic footwear increased as consumers' incomes increased (see Table 7.2). Market research for 1998 indicated that people in Shanghai owned only one pair of athletic footwear. By 2005, they had, on average, three pairs. In terms of style, people's preferences changed from choosing footwear for functional purposes to opting for fashion. Athletic footwear retailers selling name-brand shoes had what seemed to be a promising future.

Table 7.2 Consumption of Recreation Goods in Entertainment and Sports Sector, 1997–2004

	1997	1998	1999	2000	2001	2002	2003	2004
Per Capital Annual Disposable Income of Urban Households								
Income	5,160.3	5,425.1	5,854.0	6,280.0	6,859.6	7,702.8	8,472.2	9,421.6
Per Capital Annual Living Expenditures for Consumption in Sector of Education, Culture, and Recreation Service								
Consumption	448.38	499.39	567.05	669.58	736.63	902.28	934.38	1,032.80

Source: China Statistics Yearbooks (various years).

The Glorious Age

The success of his first store encouraged Wang to open more stores, more quickly than he had initially planned. In the months following his franchise premiere in Shanghai in 1998, Wang adopted an aggressive expansion strategy, opening a new store every 22 days. After spreading the business to the North China region, the company opened 40 corporate stores in seven other Chinese cities. The company realized a profit in its second year of operations, reaching a sales volume of US$14 million in 2000.

Every one of RetailCo's stores acted in accord with the global standard of The Athlete's Foot, Inc. The stores, equipped with indoor music, sports videos, and fashionable designs, established a pleasant atmosphere for shopping. All stores provided the best possible service for their customers. The service staff in every store were trained before they began their work—also in accordance with the model that Wang and his team had seen in Atlanta. In addition, every store was equipped with computers for billing and inventory control. In fact, the inventory-control system was an advantage that distinguished Wang's stores from other retailers. By adhering to strict, computerized tracking of products, store managers were able to react promptly to shortages or excesses of inventory. The company used the franchisor's proprietary pricing model by utilizing aggressive price reductions to manage inventory excesses. More important than the store brands that the store marketed were the famous internationally branded sports goods, such as Nike, Adidas, and Reebok, which were available at the stores. A pioneering store atmosphere, an excellent inventory-management model, and the availability of famous brands quickly made The Athlete's Foot a premier competitor in the Chinese sports retailing industry.

Domestic promotion of The Athlete's Foot brand name was also managed aggressively. Besides media advertising, the company put more emphasis on direct and in-store marketing. It organized three-on-three street basketball games and tournaments to grab the attention of young sports lovers. The company also sponsored high-school basketball teams to further inculcate brand-name recognition of both the stores and their products among teenagers. In-store marketing activities included cooperation with the fast-food giant, McDonald's; monthly newsletters advertising The Athlete's Foot were distributed in McDonald's stores. Nevertheless, the brand-building process was not as successful as it had been in the United States. People responded to the brands of products more than to the retail brand itself: Consumers visited stores because they could find internationally known products, not necessarily because they were drawn to The Athlete's Foot as a brand. This customer motivation would lead to substantial problems for Wang in future years.

In 2000, Wang started, cautiously, to seek appropriate franchisees in an attempt to expand the business. Wang selected one sporting goods franchising exhibition in Beijing as the venue for promotion of his franchise opportunities. Almost 500 applicants applied for franchises in one day, far exceeding Wang's expectations. Some applicants even came with large amounts of cash as testament to their financial abilities (and solvency). Wang was concerned, however, about the values of the applicants; he wanted to ensure that the selected candidates were service-oriented and fully understood the partnership requirements related to franchising. Carefully vetting all of the applicants, Wang short-listed 20 candidates. These finalists had strong financial capabilities as well as fine educational backgrounds; they could understand the vital realities involved in franchising partnerships. RetailCo invited these 20 candidates to come to the Shanghai Office for face-to-face meetings with the board. Finally, one—out of 500—was signed with RetailCo to be the first subfranchisee of The Athlete's Foot, Inc. Later, using the same careful scrutiny, 12 additional subfranchisee stores were developed in second- and third-tier cities, such as Nanjing, Wuxi, and Ningbo.

Signs of Problems

In 2001, in spite of—or possibly due to—its rapid growth, the company gradually felt pressures related to cash flow, marketing, and supply. The first "pressure" came from the need to commit large amounts of capital to obtaining retail venues. Because the location of retail stores was related to sales' performance, gaining a quality location was crucial. Wang's good fortune in being able to open his first store at a high-traffic, upscale shopping area in Shanghai was often difficult to replicate at equally moderate rental rates. Obtaining a quality retail space in China usually requires at least a 24-month leasing commitment; in some department stores, a 36-month rental agreement was the norm. To lock in quality locations in this competitive a retail real-estate market, the company signed long-term contracts, looking to best competitors by securing desirable locations. This laudable approach to ensuring franchisee success, however, required an immense commitment of up-front capital. RetailCo took over prime spaces in department stores, but the cost of doing so was great. Unfortunately, when market conditions changed and sales decreased, the pressure caused by an insufficiency of ready reserves of cash inevitably increased.

A second pressure was related to a problem many "breakthrough" franchisors experience in new markets: Since 2001, The Athlete's Foot had started to lose its "first-mover" advantage. China began in 2000 to finalize preparations for entry into the WTO. The global financial community was increasingly convinced by then that the immense potential of the Chinese market was soon to become a reality. As a result, the athletic footwear market—along with every other foreign franchise business—underwent major changes, and foreign direct investment (FDI) increased.

In department stores, the space for sporting goods enlarged dramatically from 300 square meters to 700 square meters, then to 1,000, to 1,500, and, finally, to an average of 3,000 square meters. This growth spurt meant that franchising space allotted to The Athlete's Foot was, as a percentage of total space, gradually diminished. More footwear retailing players joined the industry; for example, Quest Sports started to open stores in China in 2001. Competition also came from local players, who were able to insinuate themselves in this market due to competitive pricing, enhanced customer service, and increased product quality. In other words, these local competitors learned from Wang's The Athlete's Foot franchises what Wang had learned from the franchisor. A final concern occurred when individual brands opened more of their own stores.

As a result of its success in the market—partly related to the improved business climate in China as a whole—RetailCo/The Athlete's Foot was, paradoxically, losing its competitive advantage. In 1998, the size of The Athlete's Foot store was almost 100 square meters, often occupying one-third of the total size of the sporting goods section of a large department store. The typical store was supplied by several world-famous brands, such as Nike, Adidas, and Reebok. The rest of the sporting goods space was devoted to selling locally branded products and sports equipments: footballs, basketballs, tennis rackets, and so on. Although the goods sold in The Athlete's Foot store were exclusive and superior to others, the above-mentioned changes led to a tenfold increase in the amount of store space devoted to sporting goods. The Athlete's Foot did not and could not grow as fast, now (post-2001) occupying merely one-fifteenth of the total space devoted to sporting goods in a large department store. Size and visibility matter: The "idea" of The Athlete's Foot became increasingly insignificant in customers' minds.

Worse, for Wang, was the fact that his suppliers—the producers of the often-popular styles and models his growing customer base demanded—began to increase their own penetration of what had previously been a fairly wide-open market. The Athlete's Foot multibrand approach was forced to compete directly with brand-name suppliers who opened their own outlets in direct competition. Inevitably, Wang found it difficult to get the most desirable brand-name products for his stores; the home office—although committed to Wang's status as the master franchisor—was unable to put enough pressure on producers to stem the tide. Wang's stores were unable to keep current inventory of the most recent styles and most in-demand products.

With declines of comparative store size and product varieties, and increases in competition from local and brand-specific market entrants, The Athlete's Foot found itself squeezed out of high-value department store venues. Department stores welcomed the single-brand retailers because they were content with the smaller ratios of retail space; besides, grouping single-brand retailers together made a department store one, huge multibrand store. The Athlete's Foot had to move to street-front locations that commanded higher rents and were less popular with the purchasing public. Thus, costs increased but revenue decreased.

What Should Wang Do?

Rick Wang realized the company was in risk of bankruptcy if he did not immediately address the radically changed demands of the marketplace. The available options and Wang's decisions and actions are discussed in Chapter 8.

Endnotes

1. According to The Athlete's Foot, Inc., the FitPrint System is a proprietary state-of-the-art computerized technology that measures pressure points at different phases of a customer's gait.

2. www.theathletesfoot.com (accessed July, 2005).

3. Ye-Sho Chen, "Franchise China: She is Ready, Are You?," http://isds.bus.lsu.edu/chen/Franchise.htm (accessed July 2005).

4. *Franchise: The International and Management of Franchise*, Xinhua Press, Beijing, 2003, pp. 181.

5. Ibid.

8

Master International Franchising in China: The Athlete's Foot (Part B)

Amber Xu, Ilan Alon

In a quickly changing market, Rick Wang and his Athlete's Foot stores encountered a series of problems that threatened his company. Increased competition, in what had heretofore been an "open" market, forced Wang to work out a number of strategies so that his franchise plans could survive. After evaluating and implementing a number of strategies, Wang made a difficult decision. The available options and Rick Wang's actual decisions are discussed in the following case study.

A Struggle for Survival

After being squeezed out of department stores by his competitors, Wang had to relocate his business to "the street" or to less-desirable, lower-traffic shopping malls in order to adhere to a certain economy of scale. However, the consequences of his decision to relocate led to higher rents and lower sales. Wang was forced into a string of strategic decisions, all related to stricter competition from better-positioned competitors. In fact, Wang faced a retailer's worst nightmare: higher costs and lower profits. Worse still, the more stores he had, the worse his bottom line fared—despite the fact that rapid franchise growth had been his key strategy before competitors emerged in his market. Ultimately, Wang had to close stores to preserve the financial balance of his overextended empire.

When Wang looked for alternative retailing methods, ones which would complement his established but faltering onsite retailing outlets, he opted for e-commerce. He wondered if selling shoes in a virtual store would lead to increased profits and act as a magnet for his brick-and-mortar operations. He "opened" an online shoe booth aimed at reclaiming and increasing consumers' brand loyalty to his product.

Unfortunately, the online booth did not succeed in attracting customers. E-commerce, at that time, was in its infancy in China, though it was booming in most Western countries. Limited by uncertain Internet access and restrained by a lack of credit, consumers in this section of the Chinese market were not (yet) comfortable with Internet retailing. Additionally, Chinese consumers were culturally attuned to the physical act of "trying and buying." And, because Wang's products were quite expensive when compared with local athletic shoes, he also had to overcome a cultural distaste for purchasing items by virtue of appearance alone. Even major international suppliers of competitors' footwear brands had rejected online marketing, so Wang's choice—although a forward-looking one—was not something that more experienced retailers had found useful.

In athletic footwear retailing, having the most fashionable and trendy supply is essential. Wang turned to his franchisor, The Athlete's Foot, Inc., to help him with local supply-chain problems. He assumed that his franchisor, with its 30-year history of international experience (including stores in over 40 countries) would help him to overcome his lack of leverage over reluctant suppliers. He assumed incorrectly.

The franchisor was simply not as well informed and powerful in this market as Wang had hoped. The Athlete's Foot, Inc., had been successful in the American domestic market, and had also done well in Australia and parts of Europe; however, it had almost no substantive experience in or knowledge of the Chinese market. The Athlete's Foot, Inc., did support Wang by providing an efficient business model, a superior operations system, and some basic retailing knowledge, but this was all they could offer. The Athlete's Foot, Inc., did not have corporate stores in China, nor did it have any other experience in the Chinese market. Wang and his company would have to bear the sole responsibility for success in this immense and uncertain business environment.

Ironically, even while Wang's local branch stores in Shanghai were losing revenue, his subfranchisees, mostly in smaller cities like Nanjing, Wuxi, and so on, were still doing quite well. They were making profits and enjoying the results of increased customer traffic and brand consciousness. This disconnect was primarily due to a lag in the maturation of their different submarket niches. Major brands were, at that time, focusing on building market share in the larger cities, and what would come to be called the "single-brand trend" had not yet extended to those smaller cities. As was the norm in other international markets, market transformation in smaller cities tended to be 18 to 24 months behind that in the largest cities. It was for this reason that Wang's franchisees were thriving even as he faltered.

On the other hand, even as his franchisees celebrated their survival in these smaller Chinese cities, they were becoming aware—through Wang's experience—that they faced an uncertain future once the single-brand giants came to compete with them in these less-mature markets. It was likely that these profitable franchisees would come to face the same problems that Wang was encountering in his more-mature market. Current success does not guarantee future survival, so even these franchisees had an interest in Wang's strategies.

Transformation

Wang's attempts to rescue his stores from crisis had failed. To avoid bankruptcy, Rick Wang eventually made a painful decision: He would terminate his contract with the franchisor. He recalled: "I took a gamble, and I decided that we would restructure our company." He chose to convert his retailing stores from The Athlete's Foot to Adidas, from a franchising structure to a "pure" retailing operation. He chose to concentrate on single-brand rather than on multibrand retailing, following what he perceived as structural changes in the marketplace.

His decision was painful as well as adventurous. The termination of the franchising relationship could lead to costly legal action if he could not negotiate with The Athlete's Foot, Inc. He understood the need for extreme caution at this point; otherwise, the company would be beaten down before it could be rebuilt.

Calmly and carefully, Wang began the process of exiting the franchise relationship by communicating with the franchisor—always professionally—about the intricacies of the crisis facing the sports footwear market in the current Chinese environment. Wang tried to convince the franchisor that great efforts had been made to build and maintain the brand; The Athlete's Foot *could* succeed *if* there were no changes to the market that they had entered together. However, as the market changed, the retailer was forced to change its marketing strategy to deal with these changes. Wang specifically pointed to the franchisor's inability to corral suppliers, which ultimately deprived him of a responsible way to address change and guarantee the survival of The Athlete's Foot in China.

As he considered his exit strategy, Wang also communicated with his own franchisees, hoping to have them join him as he transformed his company. He made clear to the franchisees the problems he was facing—and those that they, too, would soon face: changing market trends, the reluctance of big-brand suppliers to commit, and the weaknesses of The Athlete's Foot as a franchisor. "If you want to continue with multi-brand, we will do our best to help. But you probably will not get some big brands to fully cooperate," Wang said to them. He welcomed those who committed to his future plans, and he committed himself to a parenting role as they made the move with him.

Instead of royalties and operations fees—such as those they would expect to have to pay in a standard franchising format—Wang promised to adopt a direct operational model: Those stores would become more like subdealers, buying the latest supplies from Wang and paying him a small commission derived from their sales volumes. In this way, supply-chain problems could be managed, and franchisee costs would not be fixed if sales volumes dropped. For those who were unwilling to follow, Wang chose to take over their stores, paying fair compensation in each case. Wang agreed to subsidize their depreciated inventory costs and refund them some of the money they had paid for their franchises.

Wang's openness and fairness avoided legal disputes and, even better, won the trust of most of his subfranchisees. They converted themselves to Adidas retailers, demonstrating their full confidence in Wang's leadership as together they made the transition from multi-brand to single-brand retailing.

Gradually, Wang and his company recovered from hardship: Sales volumes increased continuously and he found himself setting new sales records. Although he was no longer operating under the franchise model, Wang credits his experience with The Athlete's Foot, Inc., as a core part of his current success, recently saying:

> I still believe in the franchising model—it is a very good growth model. When it plays out properly, you can grow your business tremendously. It is regretful that changes in the market hurt my operation, and these changes prevented the system from sustaining profitability.

9

Social Entrepreneurship and Sustainable Farming in Indonesia

Ilan Alon, Eve Misati

Sitting contemplatively in his restaurant and gazing over the rice fields of *Sok-Wayah* in Ubud, Bali, Oded Carmi mulled over his options to replicate the success of his farm, *Sari Organik*—specifically, to reintroduce organic rice farming in other parts of Bali and eventually throughout Indonesia. The idea of *Sari Organik* was initially conceived in 1997 when Carmi sought to build a model farm that would grow organically with market demand and benefit the community while serving as an educational center for small-scale farmers keen to build a "green Bali."

Thirteen years later, the message of the organic farm had not been well embraced by the farmers and landholders and, as a result, diversified food production had not taken place as anticipated. Determined to rejuvenate the community's flagging enthusiasm and carry his mission to fruition, Carmi realized that he needed to analyze his options for replication and sustenance, and act fast. His initial thoughts included some options:

1. To utilize the established village system and its leadership (religious and civil) to reintroduce the traditional rice-farming culture in Ubud, Bali, and eventually Indonesia

2. To introduce a new model such as microfranchising through which he (the microfranchisor) would recruit a number of local farmers (microfranchisees) and provide them with the resources to grow rice organically

3. To go into a joint venture with the few existing organic rice farmers in the region

4. To expand his business as a sole proprietor; that is, to buy more land and increase organic rice production—this was his least favorite option because it would go against his mission of involving the community

Carmi wasn't sure which of these four options would be best and also wondered if there were other viable options that would help him achieve his mission for the *Sari Organik* farm.

Oded Carmi's Social Entrepreneurship Background

A budding social entrepreneur,[1] Carmi was born in 1950 in *Kibbutz Matsuba*, Israel, just south of the Lebanese border, barely two years after the State of Israel's declaration of independence from the British Mandate of Palestine. The *Kibbutz* was a large, collective production unit or cooperative settlement whose members jointly owned the means of production and shared social, cultural, and economic activities—however, the trend of the *Kibbutz* was now shifting from farming toward environmental business.[2] During Mr. Carmi's youth, *Kibbutz Matsuba* owned an agribusiness and provided what it considered relevant agricultural education for its children through a farm (*meshek yeladim*) where the children worked once a week instead of receiving formal schooling.

At 18 years of age, Carmi joined the Israel Defense Forces (IDF), where he worked for three years as an air traffic controller before relocating to the United States. He first settled in Washington, D.C., where he worked in sheetrock construction for 18 months before moving to Boulder, Colorado, where he continued to work in construction, and also learned to fly airplanes. After four years in Boulder, he decided to move to Los Angeles, California, but things did not turn out well there; after a nine-month stint at a horse ranch, he decided to move to New York, where he started a moving company with a friend—Carmi's first entrepreneurial venture. The moving company did not last long, so he returned to construction and also got involved in the performing arts, and later moved to San Francisco, where he lived for two years before returning to New York in 1978.

In New York, Carmi continued to work in construction, maintained his involvement in the performing arts, and later, in partnership with four friends, opened a restaurant (gallery bistro) in the East Village, which lasted four years. Carmi continued to live in New York but had a growing desire to settle elsewhere. In search for a place to call home, Carmi first visited Bali in 1992 and later visited Costa Rica and the Dominican Republic, finally getting an opportunity in 1997 when a Balinese acquaintance he had met in New York invited him to Ubud, Bali, and offered him a piece of land for free with permission to build a house.

Once he moved to Ubud, Carmi immersed himself in the Balinese way of life and embarked on subsistence farming close to the nearby river. He first experimented with a variety of organic fruits and vegetables and later organic rice and farm animals. It was at this time that his mission began to hatch—to get farmers to grow complete diets, rather than just rice, as a way to nourish the community and also alleviate poverty. For two years, he traveled back and forth between Bali and New York until his wife, who was still living in New York at the time, suddenly died in 1999, leaving behind an 18-month-old son. Carmi decided to sell the two apartments and a co-op he owned in New York and relocated permanently to Bali with his infant son.

For eight years following the death of his wife, Carmi chose to work solely for the social enhancement of others, living off his savings. He started two nongovernmental organizations (NGOs), *Senang Hati* (Happy Hearts), established in 2000 to assist people living with disabilities, and *Rainbow Mandala*, established in 2003 with a group of Israeli women to provide hope to the community through activities such as hosting special events for orphanages, donating food and presents to the needy, and hosting Christmas day activities. The latter did not last long, but the former had strong organization and had since received foreign support, and is currently operating as *The Senang Hati Foundation*.[3]

As a social entrepreneur, Carmi was passionate about the welfare of the communities in Ubud and was keen to reintroduce sustainable traditional organic rice farming with a commitment to mobilize the community to help replicate this initiative in other parts of Bali, and eventually throughout Indonesia. His dream was to see farmers in the community grow organic rice and, during rotation, use the fallow land to grow vegetables and fruits, and perhaps rear farm animals, thus providing a wholesome diet and a sustainable source of income. Rather than leave this issue to the government and business sector, Carmi realized that it was necessary to engage the local community through its religious and civil leadership to take the initiative of improving its own social and economic welfare.

Sari Organik

The name *Sari Organik* was obtained in 2005 when Carmi realized that after about eight years of experimenting with organic vegetables, he was producing more than he could sell to friends. Two years later, the wife of the landowner who had given him land for free issued him an ultimatum to start paying for the land or move out. Carmi chose to stay and decided to invest what was left of his savings (approximately $50,000) to start a small business—an organic farm and restaurant—and thus *Sari Organik* Farm and the restaurant, *Bodag Maliah* (overflowing basket), were established in December 2007.

To supplement their existing land, Carmi and his Balinese wife, Nila, who was also their restaurant's head chef, acquired more land from another friend and later befriended their mentors, the owners of "The Big Tree Farms."[4] The latter were the largest organic American expatriate farmers in Bali and the couple sought advice from them on how to turn their experimental farm into a socially responsible yet profitable venture that would enhance the community's well-being and augment the couple's dwindling savings.

Through *Sari Organik*, Carmi hoped to reestablish the severed connection between consumers and farmers, which in his opinion was engendered by how the rise of multinational corporations (MNCs) led to a disconnect between food processing and farming and posed a major threat to small-scale organic farmers. The objective of *Sari Organik* was to process food in a transparent manner, close to the consumer, thus *Sari Organik* processed and sold food directly to the consumer without middlemen, that is, wholesalers and retailers. The farm's survival was dependent upon consumers' willingness to buy the local organic produce at a slightly higher price than imported food sold by MNCs, which was a real challenge in a world where consumers were used to the MNCs' discount pricing.

Sari Organik employed 35 people as of 2010—five organic rice farmers who were involved in the growing, processing, transportation, and delivery of the farm's produce, and 30 restaurant workers involved in food processing, watering, cooking, and various restaurant functions. Besides varieties of organic rice, *Sari Organik* had produced the following products thus far: fruit jams, natural syrups, fruit wines, tofu, soy feta and soy ricotta cheeses, natural sauces, different kinds of bread, pickled products, seeds, fermented teas, and roasted nuts. The restaurant served healthy organic meals made from the farm's produce.

Carmi's goal was to keep the organic rice prices as low as possible and pay the organic rice farmers a much higher percentage of the sales price than what they would earn on their own. *Sari Organik* paid more than double the normal salary in Bali, but the work was harder because it was organic and the yield was lower because no chemicals were used—and because the land needed reconditioning after years of using harmful fertilizers. The restaurant depended on the level of tourism; during high season, it generated about 200 million rupiahs a month in revenue (before accounting for tax and expenses), with a profit of about 80 million rupiahs a month. During low season, the restaurant sometimes did not break even and Carmi had to pump in his savings. Table 9.1 shows *Sari Organik's* consolidated income statement for the month ending April 30, 2010.

Table 9.1 Consolidated Income Statement for the Month Ending April 30, 2010 (in IDR)

Revenue		
Warung Bodag Maliah (Sari Organik Restaurant)		
Sales		153,302,500
Sari Organic Café (Little tree)		
Processed products	4,801,200	
Fresh produce	262,250	5,063,450
Farmers' market—processed products		
Processed products	760,000	
Fresh produce	206,000	966,000
Sari Organik Farm		
Garden vegetables and salads	13,054,800	
Rice plantation	570,000	
Other produce	12,897,500	26,522,300
Total revenue		**185,854,250**
Expenditure		
Warung Bodag Maliah (Sari Organik Restaurant)		
Cost of goods sold		
Makro	6,819,641	
Garden vegetables and salads	13,054,800	
Rice	570,000	
Ginger juice	5,154,000	
Lemon	1,140,000	
Lemon marquisa	1,210,000	
Storm beer	3,420,000	
Other menu items	44,200,000	75,568,441

Expenditure

Equipment purchase			
	Jars	924,000	
	Food processor	450,000	
	Juicer	2,500,000	
	Blender	670,000	
	Glasses and soup bowls	1,180,000	5,724,000
Other expenses			
	Printing notes and memos	420,000	
	Menu covers	300,000	
	Central bill (promotions)	7,312,300	
	Employee salaries	21,585,250	
	Maintenance	632,000	
	Air conditioning	825,000	
	Electricity	1,100,000	32,174,550
Sari Organik Farm			
Farm workers' salaries			
	Kintamani farm	925,000	
	Others	6,982,500	7,907,500
Purchases			
	Brown rice	960,000	
	Sabu vegetables (Jan. to Mar.)	5,191,750	
	Other farm inputs	13,381,500	
	Nets and maintenance	454,000	19,987,250
Miscellaneous			
Gas, salary, phone, security, full moon offerings, advertising			19,905,000
Total expenditure			**161,266,741**
Income before tax			**24,587,509**
	Less tax	10%	2,458,751
Income after tax			**22,128,758**
			=US$2,445

Note: The exchange rate on July 3, 2010, was 9050.0194 Indonesian rupiahs (IDR) = 1 U.S. dollar.

Source: Company records.

Carmi had embraced his responsibility to manage his farm responsibly and sustainably in order to contribute to and not just exploit *Sari Organik's* stakeholders. He realized that it was vital to establish the confidence of the community at large and the village leaders (religious and civil), and even of individual farmers and consumers, to assure them that *Sari Organik* was worthy of their trust. Carmi knew that any business with a desire to survive into the future would be well advised to adopt the best practice of "sustainable development," defined by the United Nations (UN) as a process of change in which the exploitation of resources, the direction of investments, the orientation of technological development, and institutional change are all in harmony and enhance both current and future potential to meet human needs and aspirations.[5] Like MNCs and other large-scale businesses, small entrepreneurs are equally charged with the responsibility of running sustainable, responsible businesses.

As a small business owner, Carmi fulfilled his corporate social responsibility (CSR)[6] not only through the generation of employment opportunities for the community, but also through (1) the provision of an educational and nurturing work environment for his employees (*Sari Organik* was a model farm for the community); (2) the sustainable use of land and agricultural resources (he did not use fertilizers, but instead used animal manure and organic composts to fertilize the soil, and also strived to maintain the ecological balance of his land through biodiversity, leaving animals such as snakes, eels, frogs, fish, dragonflies, freshwater crabs, and a variety of insects in their natural habitats in the rice fields so that they could contribute to the health of the soil and water systems); (3) allowing his land to lie fallow from time to time to prevent exhaustion and rotating the crops to replace depleted nitrogen in the soil; and (4) the sales of healthy, nutritious organic ware from his farm to the community at reasonable prices.

The Environment: Indonesia

Home to the world's largest Muslim population, Indonesia gained its independence from the Netherlands in 1949, but only held its first free parliamentary general elections in 1999, ending a repressive rule. Indonesia was also the third-largest democracy after India and the United States, respectively, the fourth most populous country in the world (approximately 242 million)[7] after China, India, and the United States, respectively, and the world's largest archipelagic state (about three times the size of Texas). According to Worldwide Governance Indicators (WGI) for 2008,[8] Indonesia ranked in the 10th to 25th percentile on political stability, and ranked in the 25th to 50th percentile on voice and accountability, government effectiveness, regulatory quality, rule of law, and control of corruption. The Indonesian government was involved in legal and economic reforms and had shown a remarkable turnaround under President Susilo Bambang Yudhoyono's watch.

A highly collectivist society, Indonesia ranked as follows on Hofstede's cultural dimensions:[9] 78 on power distance (United States, 40), 48 on uncertainty avoidance (United States, 46), 14 on individualism (United States, 91), and 46 on masculinity (United States, 62). Doing business in this society required patience and an understanding of the influences affecting business culture and the legal and regulatory environments. The country was facing challenges with issues such as poverty, unemployment, inadequate infrastructure, underdeveloped education, corruption, and a complex regulatory environment, among others. The economy was emerging: 52% of its population lived in urban areas, with an annual urban growth rate of 3.3%. Agriculture contributed 42% to Indonesia's labor workforce, while industry contributed 18% and services contributed 39%. Indonesia was industrializing, but remained an agrarian society in transition. Indonesian economic growth relied mainly on domestic consumption, and its GDP had been increasing (ranked 16th in the world with PPP at $969 billion, 33rd with a real growth rate at 4.5%, and 155th with per capita PPP at $4,000[10]), with agriculture contributing 15%, industry contributing 47%, and services contributing 37%, as of 2009.[11]

A developing country, Indonesia was also facing a number of environmental challenges, including deforestation, water pollution from industrial waste, sewage, air pollution in urban areas, smoke and haze from forest fires, and so on. The country boasted a sophisticated irrigation system covering 45,000 square kilometers of land, with only 11% arable land. There was a dire need for sustainable development (going green) in order to manage the natural resources that would reduce poverty and support human development.

Rice Farming in Bali

Research into the history of rice farming in Bali indicates that Bali had been producing rice for more than 1,100 years.[12] The region originally grew a variety of rice grains, each with a distinct flavor, texture, aroma, and even color: pink, white, brown, red, and black. All farming was originally done with no harmful chemicals, using only natural compost and animal manure. The "Green Revolution"[13] was launched in Indonesia in the late 1960s over concerns of food security in the country. The Indonesian government, with the help of the World Bank, developed a grain rice hybrid that was supposed to give a higher yield and, therefore, increase the productivity of farmers. Government mandates to use the new rice variety as well as related pesticides and chemicals led to increased production and Indonesia became agriculturally independent, making enough rice to feed itself. Short-run gains, however, were difficult to maintain in the long run as the ill effects of the policy were not fully foreseen.[14]

To continue this trend, the use of chemicals and pesticides was intensified while the use of animal manures and organic composts slowly stopped. This led to deprivation of the soil of rich natural ingredients over the years, and eventually rice yields and quality began to decline even with the intensified use of chemicals; farmers thought they could turn things around by using even more chemicals and fertilizers and this increased the costs of producing rice, while the yields continued to decline and the supply could not meet demand anymore—leading to the need for the country to import rice through MNCs in 1985.

The use of chemicals upset the ecological balance and destroyed biodiversity as animals and insects died from the harmful chemicals. Although not substantiated in the case, it is likely that those chemicals and fertilizers may also have affected the health of the people because local farmers applied the chemicals without the use of gloves and masks for protection. The communities also depended on a single water source flowing through the rice fields, and therefore any chemicals introduced into the water system would inherently contaminate all the fields downstream. During the shift in rice farming, some farmers, especially in the remote areas, held onto a little organically grown traditional rice for their own consumption because they found the hybrid white rice odorless and tasteless. Organic rice farming became a boutique item in Bali, but a few more farmers expressed interest in shifting to this practice. The initial yields were disheartening as the soil had been contaminated over the years and would need reconditioning before it could produce yields to match its original level.

Growing rice without chemical inputs could save the farmers money, but they had to be willing to recondition their farms, a process that could take about 18 months according to one American expat farmer who had tried it successfully. Once the land was reconditioned, the yields were great, but the crops had to be rotated and the land made fallow between harvests in order to sustain rice farming. There were indications that the government was supportive of such initiatives by farmers in the local communities as demonstrated by the "go organic campaign" launched in 2001 to develop a certification system, give incentives to farmers developing organic farming techniques, promote the concept of organic farming through training and workshops, and provide financial assistance to farmers to enable them to build organic fertilizer processing equipment.[15] Table 9.2 provides additional key facts on general and organic farming in Bali.

Table 9.2 Farming in Bali—Key Facts

Farming in General	Organic Farming
Bali has the ideal conditions for agriculture: climate—dry and wet season, fertile soil, and availability of abundant water for irrigation.	Organic farming promotes healthy, wholesome eating for the community.
In 2009, Bali only had 228,153 hectares of fertile rice fields left. Various housing and hotel construction projects have been eating up at least 700 hectares of fertile rice fields every year.[16]	Organic farming promotes the local economy and community awareness of social entrepreneurship and sustainable development.
About 80% of Bali's economy depends on tourism—which some consider a threat to farming in the region.	About 40 years ago, most farming was organic, then the government/World Bank started to promote the use of chemicals to increase output.
Agriculture, however, is still Bali's biggest employer; specifically, rice cultivation.	Organic farming is more labor-intensive, has lower output, and is relatively expensive.
Other agricultural outputs include fruits, vegetables, Arabica coffee, fish, tuna, seaweed, vanilla, cattle/dairy, goats, sheep, and poultry.	The Bali Organic Association (BOA)[18] exists but isn't well developed yet.
Farming is dependent on the traditional farming system, *Subak Abian*, based on the Hindu philosophy of *Tri Hita Karana* (God, other people, and the environment), and about 93.8% of Bali's population adheres to Balinese Hinduism.	Organic farms include The Organic Farm—Bali, Big Tree Farms (Island Organics), *Sari Organik*, and Pegasus Farm. Organic Farmers' Markets held in Ubud and Sanur provide an opportunity for growers and businesses to sell their organic wares.
Bali's administration is developing 40 integrated farming sites to promote both new farming technology and traditional farming systems.[17]	A sustainable agriculture project—System of Rice Intensification (SRI)[19] has been funded by The Funding Network (TFN) through the Rotary club to train farmers on how to grow rice organically and the social and economic benefits of doing so.

The Village System in Bali

Bali was made up of basic territorial units or villages known as *Desa* (the equivalent of a city in the United States). Desa covered both the wetland where rice is grown and the dry land that consisted of compounds, gardens, temples, and roads. Each wetland had a corresponding irrigation unit known as *Subak*. Bali's equivalence of the city's suburbs was called *Banjar*. Each *Banjar* had its temples and organizations. A *Banjar's* basic social unit was the couple (*pekurenan*); only married couples were full members of the *Banjar* and were subject to *Banjar* rights and obligations. Decisions were taken by the male members of the social unit and passed after reaching unanimity. The *Banjar* made up an association called the *Banjar suka duka* (the association for the sharing of joy and pain), whose bonds were arguably the most important of all in the network of village associations. Each *Banjar* was made up of anything between fifty and two hundred individual compounds, and in every *Banjar* there were two main leaders, one religious (*Kelian Adat*) and one civilian (*Kelian Dinas*, who sometimes doubled as the village headman, *Bendesa Adat*).[20]

Civilian leaders were either elected or appointed by the villagers, while the religious leader was chosen by village elders. Since 1979, the *Banjar* had been recognized as the lowest administrative structure of the national Indonesian administration, directly under the authority of the *perbekel* or *lurah* (village head) and beyond the traditional village headman (*Bendesa Adat*). In many villages, elders were used to settle disputes, and in many communities in Bali, where Hinduism permeated lifestyles, religious leaders had great power and influence over civilian leaders, whose main responsibilities were to issue ID cards, marriage certificates, death certificates, land rights use, and approvals for construction. The Balinese had a respect for authority, and were used to following their leaders' orders.

About 93.8% of Bali's population adhered to Balinese Hinduism—a combination of the existing local beliefs and Hindu influences from South Asia and South East Asia. As a result, Balinese Hinduism had a strong influence on the Balinese way of life; most notable was the deeply entrenched concept of *Tri Hita Karana* (*Tri* means "three," *Hita* means "well-being," and *Karana* means "cause"). This concept promoted a harmonious relationship among the spiritual, social, and natural environments based on the belief that such harmony generated a maximum benefit to human spiritual, mental, and physical well-being.[21] Organic farming promoted a relationship similar to that of the *Tri Hita Karana* philosophy, and if the community leaders chose to use this philosophy to increase awareness of the benefits of organic farming, the community would undoubtedly follow.

Bali experienced a tropical climate all year, with two main seasons: dry (April to September) and wet (October to March). To sustain their rice paddies during the dry season, the Balinese had used community rice-growing associations (*Subaks*), which utilized a water irrigation system, for hundreds of years. *Subaks* aimed to ensure that the water was fairly distributed to all farmers during the dry season and *Subaks* had been considered a foundation of society in Bali, headed by a respected elected leader, *Kelian Subak*.

Subak members had equal rights, regardless of caste or title or the size of their land holding, and worked together to bring water from sometimes distant sources, for example, springs, rivers, or lakes, through sophisticated hydraulic engineering systems that consisted of continuously maintained, hand-built aqueducts, small dams, canals, and underground tunnels dug through solid rock. The *Subak* met monthly under the leadership of the *Kelian Subak*, and together they decided all issues concerning rice cultivation, for example, planting, harvesting, offerings, ceremonies, repairing dams, fertilizing, and so forth; the *Kelian Subak* had the authority to grant or withhold permission for new rice terrace construction, and was responsible for ensuring compliance with government regulations.[22]

Modern life had infiltrated the community, and nobody desired to be a farmer because of the low status and minimal income associated with this profession; farmers were not respected.[23] Despite the "modernization" of agriculture in Indonesia, certain traditions held; from Carmi's balcony, farmers could be seen using their ancestors' farming techniques, for example, the use of hand tools to till the land.

Ubud, Bali, Indonesia

A beautiful town located amongst rice paddies and steep ravines in the middle of the island of Bali, Ubud was one of the island's major fine arts and cultural centers and was supported largely by tourism—from backpackers to art connoisseurs, the town drew people who were actively involved in art, nature, anthropology, music, dance, architecture, environmentalism, and "alternative modalities," among others, and boasted scenic rice fields, small villages, arts and crafts communities, ancient temples, palaces, rivers, and cooler temperatures than the main tourist area in Southern Bali. Ubud provided accommodation and dining ranging from small boutique hotels to more elegant hotels. The town derived its name from the Balinese word *"ubad"* (medicine), as the region was originally an important source of medicinal herbs and plants.[24]

About 80% of Bali's economy came from tourism, although agriculture (mostly rice cultivation) was still Bali's biggest employer. The government saw these two industries as a way to raise money through taxes.[25] *Sari Organik's* model was not well embraced and Carmi speculated that one of the reasons could be that rice farming did not generate much income for the farmers anymore due to land overuse and destruction of top soil from the use of harmful chemicals. Hence, about 90% of farmers had second jobs, and only dedicated a bare minimum of effort to farming just to get their share of the rice. For every eight sacks of rice, one went to the picker or harvester, 3.5 went to the landowner, and 3.5 went to the farmer—this was only enough to feed a landowner/farmer's family, without much left to sell. The other reason that *Sari Organik's* model was not well embraced could have been that farming was not considered a respectable profession due to the "dirty" nature of the work, and because many people preferred an office job over working out in the fields.

Sari Organik Striving for a Green Bali

Even though *Sari Organik* was established as a model to demonstrate this sustainable technique for local farmers to emulate, the effect had been very minimal and quite disappointing. As Carmi strove to realize his dreams of alleviating poverty and encouraging healthy, wholesome eating in Bali and eventually Indonesia at large through *Sari Organik's* socially responsible business model, he realized that he had a lot to consider. It was clear that certain changes had to be implemented, but it was not clear which changes.

After being visited by an American University expert on franchising, Carmi wondered if microfranchising could be used to reproduce the success of his farm in other parts of Indonesia.[26] Microfranchising models proliferated in the emerging markets and with social causes geared toward development.[27] Microfranchising had its roots in the modern concept of franchising, where the knowledge and concept were transferred to a local entrepreneur, who was typically from a low-income bracket, to implement a business practice that would sustain the individual and the local community.

One researcher, Hoyt Edge,[28] indicated that there was a growing movement of people who would like to readopt traditional rice-farming practices. Bali was a place in the world where a cultural argument for change could work because the community's culture was so deeply rooted in religion and tradition that the people considered it second nature; every person willingly followed strict civil and religious rules known as *Adat*[29] (the rules required one to live and act rightly, fulfill one's secular and religious duties, live with grace and honor, and follow the customs of the family, village, and land).

According to Carmi, the *Subak* system was no longer functioning effectively and the atmosphere was competitive rather than cooperative; everyone was on their own, leading farmers to fight over water or guard water flowing into their farms late into the night. However, Carmi was confident that with the help of the village system's civil and religious leadership in reestablishing the *Tri Hita Karana* philosophy, things could be turned around.

Carmi's objective was to replicate this organic rice-farming model in as many parts of Bali as possible and eventually diversify throughout Indonesia, and he realized that he had to weigh the available options fast. His initial thoughts included (1) utilizing the village system and its religious and civil leadership to increase awareness of the benefits of organic rice farming and reinvigorate community interest in *Sari Organik's* model—Carmi wondered whether this initiative would be as successful as a similar undertaking that had mobilized a nearby village for the purpose of healing by cultural activity[30] through a month-long event featuring health seminars and activities related to the environment, for example, competitions by *Banjars* to clean up their streets and maintain their public garden areas; (2) adopting a model such as microfranchising that would pull in microentrepreneurs; (3) going into a joint venture with the few organic rice farmers in the region; and/or (4) finding ways to expand his own business as a sole proprietor, although this was his least favorite option. Carmi also wondered whether there could be other viable options that might help him fulfill his mission for *Sari Organik* and, more generally, organic farming in Indonesia.

Endnotes

1. Ashoka.org defines social entrepreneurs as people who have innovative solutions to social problems and the potential to change patterns across society by demonstrating unrivaled commitment to bold new ideas. Social entrepreneurs prove that compassion, creativity, and collaboration are tremendous forces for change. See www.ashoka.org/social_entrepreneur (accessed July 1, 2010).

2. "Israel's Kibbutzim Shift from Red to Green," www.business-week.com/smallbiz/content/jun2010/sb20100623_004082.htm (accessed July 1, 2010).

3. See Senang Hati Foundation, www.senanghati.org (accessed July 1, 2010).

4. See Big Tree Farms, www.bigtreefarms.com/story (accessed July 1, 2010).

5. "Towards Sustainable Development," www.un-documents.net/ocf-02.htm#I (accessed July 1, 2010).

6. Corporate social responsibility may be defined as any activity that promotes the welfare of a business corporation's stakeholders; this includes philanthropic programs targeting employees and the community, commitment to promote suppliers' welfare, and other activities designed to promote environmental stewardship (sustainability).

   See Ludescher and Mashud, "CSR Exposed," *The Independent Review* 15:1 (2010): 123.

7. CIA World Factbook, 2009.

8. http://info.worldbank.org/governance/wgi/sc_chart.asp (accessed July 1, 2010).

9. www.geert-hofstede.com/hofstede_indonesia.shtml (accessed July 1, 2010).

10. CIA World Factbook, 2009

11. Ibid.

12. C. Wheeler, "A Bowl of Honest Rice," in Tales from Rural Bali, *2nd edition*, (Indonesia: Tokay Press, 2009), 199–206.

13. Green Revolution refers to the renovation of agricultural practices that began in Mexico in the 1940s. Due to its success in producing more agricultural products there, Green Revolution technologies spread worldwide in the 1950s and 1960s, significantly increasing the amount of calories produced per acre of agriculture. See http://geography.about.com/od/globalproblemsandissues/a/greenrevolution.htm (accessed July 10, 2010).

14. Economists call these ill effects negative externalities.

15. "Indonesia—The Organic Boom," www.meattradenewsdaily.co.uk/news/070610/indonesia___the_organic_boom_.aspx (accessed July 10, 2010).

16. www.indonesiaorganic.com/detail.php?id=199&cat=12 (accessed July 10, 2010).

17. www.thejakartapost.com/news/2010/02/10/bali-administration-develops-40-integrated-farming-sites.html (accessed July 10, 2010).

18. www.indonesiaorganic.com/detail.php?id=37&cat=21 (accessed July 10, 2010).

19. www.rotaryubud.org/projects/susAg-project.htm (accessed July 10, 2010).

20. http://balimagic.com/BaliAdat.html (accessed May 28, 2011).

21. Bali Tri Hita Karana, www.balitrihitakarana.com/abouttrihita-karana.htm (accessed July 1, 2010).

22. "Subak—Bali Irrigation System," www.balitravelportal.com/bali/indonesia/travel/culture/subak-bali-irrigation-system (accessed July 1, 2010).

23. C. Wheeler, "Respect," in Tales from Rural Bali, *2nd edition*, (Indonesia: Tokay Press, 2009), 271–273.

24. Scores of holistic medicine practitioners lived around Ubud, and many spas and meditation centers had opened up. One could easily find all types of Eastern and Western massage centers, reiki healers, herbal medicine shops, and even acupuncture practitioners in this town. See "Things To Do in Ubud, Bali," http://goseasia.about.com/od/bali/tp/8_things_to_do_in_ubud_bali.htm (accessed July 1, 2010).

25. www.balidiscovery.com/messages/message.asp?Id=6824 (accessed May 10, 2011).

26. Microfranchising is an economic development tool aimed to provide sound business opportunities and services to the poor by introducing scaled-down business concepts found in successful franchise organizations with the overall objective of promoting economic development by developing sound business models that can be replicated by microentrepreneurs at the base of the pyramid. See http://marriottschool.byu.edu/selfreliance/microfranchise/about (accessed July 1, 2010).

27. www.acumenfund.org/uploads/assets/documents/Microfranchising_Working%20Paper_XoYB6sZ5.pdf (accessed April 10, 2011).

28. An interview with Dr. Edge, Rollins College; see profile at http://web.rollins.edu/~hedge (accessed July 8, 2010).

29. "Bali Adat," www.balimagic.com/BaliAdat.html (accessed July 10, 2010).

30. http://news.ubud.com/2006/07/first-ubud-festival.html (accessed July 10, 2010).

10

Final Reflections and Epilogues

This book presents seven cases on franchise, emerging markets, and global operations, with multiple countries and industries represented. The analysis in the various cases also involved the context of both developed countries and developing countries and the points of view of the franchisor and the franchisee. Dividing the chapters into a 2 × 2 framework (see Table 10.1), we can see the focus of this book on cases involving franchisors in developing countries (Chapters 2, 5, and 9, "San Francisco Coffee House: An American-Style Franchise in Croatia," "Estimating Demand in Emerging Markets for Kodak Express," and "Social Entrepreneurship and Sustainable Farming in Indonesia," respectively), including Croatia and Indonesia, and demand analysis across multiple emerging markets. The master franchisee perspective is analyzed in Chapters 7 and 8 ("Master International Franchising in China: The Athlete's Foot, Inc. (Part A)" and "Master International Franchising in China: The Athlete's Foot, Inc. (Part B)," respectively), focusing on the Chinese market. Altogether, five chapters examine various developing countries and emerging markets, where franchising future potential for growth is high, due to increasing incomes, implementation of rule of law, westernization of tastes, and higher levels of urbanization.

Table 10.1 Chapter Framework

	Franchisor	**Franchisee**
Developed Country	Chapter 4, "International Marketing and Franchising at Marks & Spencer"	Chapter 3, "Trying to Create a Stir: Opening a Coffee Shop in Korea"
	Chapter 6, "Ruth's Chris Steak House: The High Stakes of International Expansion"	
Developing Country	Chapter 2, "San Francisco Coffee House: An American-Style Franchise in Croatia"	Chapter 7, "Master International Franchising in China: The Athlete's Foot, Inc. (Part A)"
	Chapter 5, "Estimating Demand in Emerging Markets for Kodak Express"	Chapter 8, "Master International Franchising in China: The Athlete's Foot, Inc. (Part B)"
	Chapter 9, "Social Entrepreneurship and Sustainable Farming in Indonesia"	

Among the developed markets, the franchisors' perspectives are also considered in Chapters 4 and 6 ("International Marketing and Franchising at Marks & Spencer" and "Ruth's Chris Steak House: The High Stakes of International Expansion," respectively). Cases on M&S from the UK and Ruth's Chris from the U.S. provide an outlook on how franchisors internationalize. In the case of M&S, franchising is used in ex-colonies and in international markets that have a demand but also face some risk or a small market. In the case of Ruth's Chris, franchising was the sole method for the company's globalization strategy. Location and partner selection was, thus, critical to the success of the brand. Chapter 3, "Trying to Create a Stir: Opening a Coffee Shop in Korea," is the only one examining how a franchisee from Korea would examine a franchising opportunity in the coffee shop industry. A review of the case synopsis, analysis, and epilogue is given for each case next.

Chapter 2: San Francisco Coffee House

Denis Tensek (MBA) and his wife, Jasmina Pacek (MFA), decided to open their own coffee house, one that was unique to the Croatian environment—a California-style coffee house that would offer the quality, service, product assortment, ambiance, and efficiency found in sophisticated coffee shops in developed markets, and all for a locally affordable price. The major challenge faced by Tensek and Pacek was how to grow. Specifically, should they consider franchising over organic growth? If so, how should they go about franchising in a country where the market is developing and where franchising is underregulated, underdeveloped, and misunderstood?

The Croatian entrepreneurs understood the benefits of franchising:

- Sharing marketing and developmental expenditures
- Developing potential of rapid development through successful duplication
- Developing economies of scale (i.e., purchasing, marketing)
- Increasing power against suppliers due to bulk purchases
- Enhancing brand through scale development
- Obtaining additional capital through fees, royalties, and/or supplies
- Externalizing development risks by reducing investment capital needed
- Lowering need for monitoring due to self-motivation of franchisee
- Becoming sole supplier of franchises, thus having monopoly power
- Coordinating vertical and horizontal channels
- Utilizing franchisees' local know-how, innovative capacity, managerial, labor, and capital resources

Despite the many advantages of franchising, franchising is not without costs. Among the problematic issues facing franchisors are:

- Monitoring difficulties across remote locations
- Possible brand name damage due to franchisee action
- Location differences in culture, economy, and purchasing behavior may limit duplication possibility
- Difficulties getting paid (i.e., royalties, advertising, supplies)
- Conflicts with franchisees; franchisees gain in power with collective power
- Possible shirking of revenue sharing
- Knowledge transfer may be expropriated
- Franchisee may become future competitor
- Buybacks of franchisees may be more expensive
- Franchisees may resist change, limiting flexibility (i.e., changing store layout)
- Potential for channel conflict
- Some differences in incentives for both parties (i.e., territory, product assortment, operations, exclusivity, etc.)
- Frequent failure due to risk of small business, loss of entire savings, and more
- Profit potential does not materialize
- Failed franchise system execution
- Competition too powerful
- Extensive litigation, political/legal intervention

To franchise is to make the necessary evaluation of the benefits and costs of such an expansion. Tensek and Pacek decided to go the franchising route despite the difficulties they would face in doing so. There were no local consultants, but through the Center of Franchising in Osijek and a USAID grant for the development of franchising in Croatia, which invited foreign experts, the entrepreneurs got the necessary know-how in developing the franchise concept. In 2006, they developed a franchise offer and sought their first franchisee, in Split.

Croatia was a developing country with a young market economy. The institutional environment, economic climate, and political transition resembled those in other Balkans-area emerging markets. In comparison to U.S. franchise laws and regulations, Croatian ones were vague or nonexistent. There was no "A to Z" on how to get things registered or legal. With the help of the local The Franchise Center in Osijek, Tensek and Pacek started their journey into discovering the ambiguous world of franchise in Croatia.

Because there was no requirement of Uniform Franchise Offering Circular (UFOC) or any similar document that would regulate the franchise offer in the market, a simple project sheet was created with the help of The Franchise Center in Osijek, specifying the San Francisco Coffee House (SFCH) franchise offer. The couple also hired a young lawyer to help them with conformity to local regulations and in preparation of a franchise contract suitable for local conditions.

The pricing was an even more important parameter due to the fact that the plan was to be put in action in the city of Osijek, situated in the region that was most impacted by the war with the Serbs, and thus was still among the least economically developed regions in the country. They did not need the financial help of banks because they relied on the franchisee capital for growth.

The first step of registering the company's name and logo as a trademark was done by the owners with the Intellectual Property Association, thus avoiding expensive lawyer's fees. To legally frame the business in terms of franchise possibilities, the couple hired a lawyer who needed to study the American franchise literature to get educated on legal issues that needed to be addressed in this kind of matter. At the same time, a Croatian lawyer was needed since a lack of the franchise regulation required familiarity with Croatian trade regulations. The lawyer they selected was able to combine elements of both in the form of a contract that was favorable to franchising.

After satisfying legal requirements, there were a number of other adjustments the owners needed to make to move SFCH from a one-shop coffee house to a chain status. First, they established a list of items that the future franchisees would have to buy from them. Because in their contract they did not specify the royalty rate as a percentage of the revenues, the owners planned to make their continuous earnings through the distribution of supplied items: coffee and aromas. These same items (coffee and aroma) ensured quality to the end customer. Only a small amount of fixed monthly fees was charged for marketing purposes.

When SFCH started in Osijek, the owners did not have their own coffee brand. Coffee cups were marked with a coffee supplier logo. Therefore, among the first steps was to create a brand, and to make their own variety of high-quality coffee blends. In collaboration with a well-established Italian roasting house, Tensek created two specific blends of coffee (SFCH Espresso blend and SFCH Mocha blend). Pacek designed unique and visually coordinated packaging that represented taste, quality, and sophistication. By doing so, they protected themselves from some possible franchisee opportunism, because SFCH was the sole supplier of its own brand. According to the franchise contract, the franchisee was obligated to buy the SFCH brand of coffee. Pacek also designed SFCH's own coffee cups and mugs, while Tensek negotiated exclusive distribution contracts with an aroma supplier.

The other coffee-related challenge for Tensek was to ensure the use of specific espresso machines and their servicing. It was a custom in Croatia that coffee suppliers provided the coffee-making machines and their service free of charge (or the cost included in the price of every kilogram of coffee).

The couple took great passion in designing the details of their brand identity: "coffee to go" packaging, staff uniform t-shirts, and

original paintings on the walls, using only certain posters and repro-
ductions. All of that became a standard that future franchise buyers
would have to follow. They created a product line that was not only
differentiated locally, but that others could not easily replicate. For
example, they did not depend on the local market for most of their
supplies. Some of the supplies were bought by the entrepreneurs
themselves in the United States and brought back to Croatia. The
entrepreneurs would also research the coffee market on their various international trips surveying the global environment for innovations in coffee retailing. The owners invested an additional €50,000 to
develop this franchise package.

Tensek and Pacek believed that their own experiences and tal-
ents uniquely differentiated them in the local market. They also had
international contacts that were difficult to imitate. Tensek flew to
America sometimes twice a year to pick up supplies and keep abreast
of competitive developments in the industry.

The Starbucks challenge was a trickier part. How could a small
local chain compete against the giant corporation? Here, too, Tensek
and Pacek had a competitive advantage. First, they knew the local;
second, Osijek was a small and remote city that would be least likely to
be targeted by multinationals; third, their price point was a lot lower
than Starbucks, making it more affordable to the local population.

To become the largest player in the country, it became clear that
national prominence was needed. SFCH local reputation grew much
media attention and, this attention, created both word of mouth about
the concept and a spillover effect on local media in new locations.
Publicity was rather simple to obtain due to some national prominence of key stories and awards the retail format received.

Tensek and Pacek quickly realized that to become a national
player, developing scale with the right franchisee partners and, perhaps, opening their own additional stores could be necessary.

SFCH opened its first franchise outlet in Split, but not after long deliberations. There were numerous requests coming to the owners of SFCH for the purchase of the franchise, but it was not until the one from Split came that they knew they had a serious buyer with the right attitude.

Below are the steps they followed in preparation for the opening of the first franchise. Those steps became their official procedure for engaging franchisees in Croatia.

1. Meeting with the owners in Osijek

The buyer interested in the purchase came to Osijek to meet with the owners and review the place in person (originally he became interested through SFCH's Web site, www.sfch.hr). Tensek and Pacek insisted that people could not be seriously interested if they did not come to the original location.

2. Discussing the size of investment and expected return

Within that first meeting, Tensek discussed basic financials that included the approximate operating costs and expected income (see Table 2.2 in Chapter 2 for an example).

3. Signing a disclosure agreement and the intent of purchase

Because the next step included going into more classified information about SFCH, Tensek and Pacek wanted to make sure that the information would stay confidential. They created a document based on the template received from the National Franchise Association in Zagreb that became their disclosure agreement as well as the intent of purchase document (with no obligation).

4. Choosing a location

Usually the prospective buyers had some sort of location in mind when thinking about buying SFCH, but after meeting with the owners, signing the disclosure agreement, and reviewing the Osijek location, they usually found that they needed to do more research. At that point, they would go back to their cities to look for what was the best available. Tensek and Pacek, for example, had several serious prospective buyers from the Croatian capital, Zagreb, who came to this point in negotiation but simply could not find the appropriate location.

In Split, the buyer hired an agency that offered him a range of locations in the city center and he took photos of all of them, e-mailing Tensek and Pacek with every option. When the choice was narrowed down to three, Tensek, Pacek, and Tanja (coffee house manager in Osijek) went to Split to help make a final selection.

5. **Fitting the shop for local space layout and developing an opening timeline**

   After the location was decided, Pacek created an adjusted "shop fitting" offer taking into consideration all the specifics of that particular location (see Table 2.3).

   The offer also specified if any adjustments were needed to the space before SFCH got involved (i.e., adjusting infrastructure, electricity, water, toilets, etc.). At that time, SFCH specified the time frame of all the activities that needed to happen before the opening.

6. **Signing a contract**

   If the above shop fitting offer was acceptable, the buyer at this point had a very specific idea of the exact size of investment, including the cost of any preparation needed before the shop fitting, the amount from the shop fitting offer, the franchise entrance fee from the contract, and the cost of the first month's lease or any other advance deposits needed for the real estate owner or agency. The contract was usually sent in advance to the buyer who had time to review it with his/her lawyer. If the total of all the costs was within the range of the investment estimated with Tensek at the first meeting and the buyer agrees to the terms, it was time to sign the franchise contract. At that point, the buyer can also sign the lease for the location, ideally for the same time period as the franchise contract.

7. Getting the work permits

The buyer then, according to the provided timeline, needed to ensure all the work permits for the new location were obtained. This is where SFCH staff helped, giving advice and recommendations.

8. Retrofitting the location

While the buyer was getting the location ready in terms of fixing the infrastructure, Pacek worked on all the shop fitting orders. When the infrastructure was ready, about a month later, the SFCH team came in to complete the shop fitting.

9. Selecting the staff

Tensek and Tanja came to Split to help the buyer select the future employees. They used their experience from Osijek to focus on specific skills and characteristics when selecting people. They made strong recommendations after interviewing the people, but the buyer made the final decision.

10. Obtaining inventory

As specified in the shop fitting offer, SFCH provided a first inventory of the main articles such as coffee and aromas, and also helped the buyer select a local supplier for all other supplies (from drinks such as water and sodas, beer and wine, to milk, sugar, toiletries, etc.).

11. Training staff

At least a week before the opening, Tanja started the intensive training with the staff. She had separate training for each workstation following the specified task list created. She had additional training for the coffee house manager and the owner (who could but did not have to be the same person). Tanja also stayed a minimum of a week after the opening to make sure all the employees were well-adjusted in their stations and that the manager and/or owner understood everything about how to run the business (working with personnel, suppliers, understanding the cash register computer system, and so on).

12. The grand opening

SFCH helped organize the opening of the new location. Local media in Osijek as well as national media in Croatia recognized the project from many angles: business newspapers and magazines as a local entrepreneurship story, interior design magazines as an example of top-of-the-line interior, and daily and lifestyle magazines as news for the local population about a new destination for their daily coffee and relaxing time. Tensek said, "We are always emphasizing the newness in the assortment: variety of choices and a great quality."

There was always a grand opening the evening before the official first day of business where VIP invitations were distributed to local businesspeople, representatives of the local establishment, and local celebrities, as well as friends and family of the local franchise unit owner. The local media (TV and press) were also invited and they usually came free of charge to cover an event such as this. So the next day, which was the first official day of business there were already stories on the local TV stations and in the local press. In addition, SFCH put up posters and gave away flyers. The first day also featured free coffee and muffin tasting (financed by the franchisee).

13. Continuous technical support and supply of goods

After the initial new unit was up and running, SFCH staff was available 24 hours a day and seven days a week for continuous technical support, which was especially important in the first few months. This turned into a partnership for the whole period of the franchise contract. As mentioned earlier, SFCH also provided a continuous supply of goods specified in the contract, on a bimonthly order basis.

Chapter 3: Coffee Franchising in Korea: A Franchisee Perspective

A critical question for entrepreneurs starting a business, particularly in a foreign country, is choosing whether or not franchising is the appropriate mode of entry. Franchising offers the entrepreneur instant brand recognition, established business processes and supply chains, regulatory and tax guidance as well as a ready supply of assistance in the early months; however, it deprives the entrepreneur of what many of them crave—the ability to create and grow a business from one's imagination. The two entrepreneurs in this case had regular salaries, but wanted to try their hands at opening a coffee shop—or a chain of coffee shops—in South Korea, which already had many brands with multiple outlets.

This case describes the challenges facing two business professors, Min-Guk "MG" Kim and Kevin Andes, who were also friends. They knew that if they bought a coffee shop franchise, they would almost certainly grow it into a successful business given their skill sets and experience; however, they also feared being a late arrival to a mature market that seemed to have commoditized the coffee shop experience. What did they need to do to set themselves apart?

Many entrepreneurs are successful because they see the future and get there first; in the United States, Bill Hewlett, Dave Packard, Bill Gates, and Michael Dell all come to mind. Other successful entrepreneurs take an existing product—coffee (Starbucks), water (Dasani), ice cream (Cold Stone), sandwiches (Panera)—and de-commoditize it; they find ways to compete based on factors other than price, and their product is often more expensive than existing market entrants.

Looking at what we know about Kim and Andes, a strengths, weaknesses, opportunities, and threats (SWOT) analysis of the team as it relates to opening a coffee shop in Korea can be instructive. Ask the students to populate the list of variables.

Strengths

- Previous entrepreneurial experience
- Business acumen
- Local knowledge of Korea
- Knowledge of and access to students, an important market segment
- Access to capital

Weaknesses

- No coffee shop management experience
- No retail experience
- Employed full-time elsewhere
- No brand awareness

Opportunities

- High current demand for the product
- Increasing demand for the product

Threats

- Tremendous competition
- Growing sense that the market has commoditized
- Price pressure in the student market

Good market selection followed by the wrong mode of entry is likely fatal to a business. Imagine choosing to enter China in 1995 to sell your high-end watches, but selecting e-commerce as the mode of entry. Likewise, poor market selection can rarely, if ever, be fixed by a good mode of entry strategy. Imagine trying to sell beer in Saudi Arabia. No mode of entry decision will rescue your business.

Differentiation strategies in Korea include:

- Location (e.g., on or near campuses)
- Cobranding with universities or university bookstores

- Combining a coffee shop with a formal or informal English-language study center
- Korean-relevant themes (e.g., sports, history, television dramas)
- Global themes (foreign cities, pictures of top-tier university campuses)
- Availability of alcohol
- Coffee types
- Coffee preparation techniques
- Food menu choices (e.g., sandwiches, desserts)
- Nonfood menu choices (e.g., tea, smoothies, hot and cold choices)
- Loyalty programs
- Partnerships with noncoffee shops

By the end of 2010, Kim and Andes decided to proceed with opening an independent coffee shop (i.e., not a franchise) on a university campus and were looking for an appropriate partner school. Their offer was that in exchange for free rent, the two would run the coffee shop and offer free English-language tutoring to student customers. The service staff would only speak English and all the signage would be only in English, giving the coffee shop the look and feel that one would find in the United States. The language tutors would be staff, the same as the coffee servers.

Chapter 4: Marks & Spencer in the UK

This case study describes the internationalization of Marks & Spencer (M&S), a giant British retailer. In recent years, the company has suffered a series of misfortunes, both at home (Britain) and abroad. Company sales have dropped, stock prices and market capitalization were substantially reduced, and overseas profits have declined. In January 1999, following a terrible earning announcement, the company announced that it had formed a marketing department, forcing the company to become more proactive and market driven. To head the department, M&S promoted James Benfield, a 17-year veteran of the retailing giant who worked as a former head of menswear, home furnishings, and direct mail.

For years, the M&S marketing philosophy was simple: Produce high-quality products under a recognized brand name at affordable (but not cheap) prices, and advertise through word of mouth. However, in recent years, this marketing philosophy has come under attack as the company started losing its competitive stance. The move to develop a marketing department was a departure from a long tradition of production/manufacturing emphasis. The problem facing James Benfield: How can M&S emerge from the slump and reposition itself as a fierce global competitor in the international marketplace?

The company's immediate response to the slowdown and the depressed stock prices has been to reduce the number of workers, decrease prices, and rethink the organization of the firm.

Job Cuts

To offset the loss in profitability, the company announced cutting 15% of its 1,900 managers in hopes of saving $16.2 million.[1] The company plans to cut an additional 350–400 head office jobs and 290 store management positions. Senior management numbers were cut by 25% (M&S Press Releases 1999). The board has been reduced from 22 to 7.[2] In addition, the company announced that it canceled its 1999 graduate trainee program, which hired about 250 graduate trainees per year, and withdrew offers made recently.[3]

Price Cuts

In an effort to become more competitive and trim down excess inventory, M&S cut prices across the board. Many clothing items, including one-third of children's wear, have been discounted by as much as 15%. The prices of one-third of all merchandise has been cut by 2% to 3%.[4]

Reorganization

M&S was reorganized into three profit centers: (1) UK retailing, (2) overseas retailing, and (3) financial services. Stores were reclassified from geographic division to four store types: (1) department stores, (2) regional centers, (3) high (main) street, and (4) small stores. The firm hopes this will help it (1) develop specific management skills associated with different store types, (2) tailor merchandise more accurately, (3) reduce administration, and (4) improve staffing and training. The total cost of restructuring is estimated at about £40 million, leading to a £40 million cost savings associated with redundancies starting in the fiscal year 2000–2001.[5]

A new marketing department was set up to help create improved (1) competitive analysis, (2) information gathering, (3) proactive communication, (4) advertising clarity, and (5) customer targeting.[6] The department will increase marketing research, develop a coherent brand strategy, and increase the level of advertising. Its marketing thrust will be to cut prices, put more staff on the shop floor, and improve visual merchandising.[7] The company will attempt to develop a more balanced sourcing policy to its domestic and international outlets and will review global logistics to streamline distribution and lower costs.[8]

The company will continue to develop their e-commerce Web site. A property division has been set up to assess use of real estate. Market cost of assets will be charged to individual stores to better assess performance. Accountability has increased as each profit center is judged individually against its cost of capital, and resources will be allocated to increase shareholders equity value.[9]

Longer term, the company needed to make more fundamental changes. The company reduced its reliance on British-made goods and developed outsourced buying centers in Hong Kong, Thailand, India, Bangladesh, Turkey, Shanghai, Italy, Indonesia, and Sri Lanka. This move was a departure from the tradition. The return-anytime guarantee was reduced to 90 days in 2005 and 35 days in 2009. In 2001, the company successfully launched a new brand *Per Una*, a clothing range designed by George Davies. The brand joined St. Michael, St. Margaret, Homecare, Orient Express, Express Tagged, and Indigo Collection brand constellation. In May 2001, the company shut down 38 European stores. By 2010, however, the number of countries which had M&S outlets has risen to 41, including Azerbaijan, Bahrain, Bermuda, Bulgaria, China, Croatia, Cyprus, Czech, Estonia, Gibraltar, Greece, Guernsey, Hong Kong, Hungary, India, Indonesia, Jersey, Kuwait, Latvia, Libya, Lithuania, Malaysia, Malta, Montenegro, Oman, Philippines, Poland, Quarter, Romania, Russia, Saudi Arabia, Serbia, Singapore, Slovakia, Slovenia, South Korea, Spain, Thailand, Turkey, Ukraine, and the United Arab Emirates. In addition to new countries, the company also experimented with new concepts including M&S Café, St Michael Food hall, home furnishing, outlet shops, and simply food.

From 1884 when the company was established until the time of the case, in the late 1990s, the company had only eight CEOs. Since 1999, the company already had five. The turnover in CEOs has increased. Comparing the financial results in the case from 1999 with the ones available in 2011, more than a decade later, suggests that the company did not make much progress in its strategy. The company, July 8, 2011 market capitalization was around $9.5 billion.[10] At the time of the case, it was around $18 billion. In contrast, Wal-Mart has a $187 billion market cap, whereas at the time of the case it was about $204 billion. In other words, while both firms lost value since 1999 in terms of market capitalization, the decline in M&S is much more substantial.

Chapter 5: Kodak Express in Emerging Markets

The Kodak case concerns an executive who must estimate the demand for Kodak Express (KE) outlets in various countries, on the basis of information from Kodak's marketing department and demographic data regarding the countries. The case requires managers to think about how to transform data on a national scale (e.g., gross domestic product per capita, population, income distribution) into a form that is meaningful for a managerial decision: the number of households in each income category. The spreadsheet model can incorporate advanced skills, such as using data tables and functions.

The objective of the case is to translate the data that are available into a form that is useful for Kodak's managers. The following data are available:

- Gross domestic product (GDP) purchasing power parity (PPP) per capita
- Population
- People per household
- Income distribution by quintile
- Kodak's criteria

The process for translating the data into another form is described in two paragraphs in the case in the section "Calculating Potential Demand." The case describes which variables influence other variables but does not direct managers regarding mathematical relationships. Managers need to spend some reflective time setting up the relationships before they begin composing a spreadsheet.

Figure 10.1 shows an influence diagram of the relationships according to the verbal description under "Calculating Potential Demand." Focus 1 in the diagram shows the steps for calculating individual income per quintile and population per quintile. These calculations will allow managers to identify the total income earned by the quintile and the average income for each person in this quintile.

Managers can then incorporate the data for people per household to determine the household income per quintile and the number of households per quintile. Focus 2 in Figure 10.1 shows the relationships. This number allows the managers to contemplate how families in the quintile are doing.

Focus 3 shows the process for counting the number of quintiles in each income category and then for calculating the number of households in each income category. Unless managers are familiar with spreadsheet functions, they may need to do these counts manually. Focus 4 shows the process for calculating the total number of Kodak Express outlets by applying the market research department's criteria to the results, that is, the company income elasticity of demand.

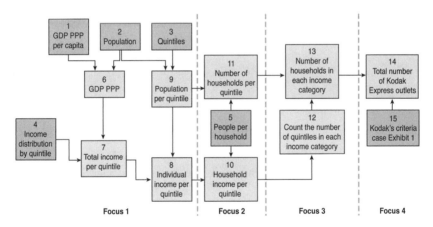

Figure 10.1 Kodak market demand assessment based on national statistics: an influence diagram

Calculating the results for 2016 requires plugging new data into the model. If the model is set up correctly, the results will change automatically. Managers will be able to see the potential growth of the market by comparing results from 2016 with results from 2010.

Chapter 6: Ruth's Chris Franchising Going Global

The first critical question facing a company's ability to grow its business internationally is where it should go next; this question is followed quickly by what mode of entry it should use and which partners it should take on. One company facing these important questions was Ruth's Chris Steak House (Ruth's Chris), the largest fine dining steak house in the United States. Ruth Fertel started Ruth's Chris in 1965 and over the next 40 years the company grew to more than 90 restaurants, about half of them franchises. Of these restaurants, only 10 were international locations.

The case describes the challenges facing Dan Hannah, vice president for business development for Ruth's Chris, as the company starts to grow its international presence following a successful initial public offering (IPO) in 2005. With restaurants in just five countries including the United States, the challenge for Hannah was to decide where to go to next.

Hannah wanted his short list to have countries in Asia, Europe, and South America. He quickly eliminated countries that were very small and very poor. Countries that were small but not poor (e.g., Bahamas) or big and poor (e.g., Vietnam) made the short list. He nominally chose the following variables to further whittle down his list:

- Beef-eaters
- Legal to import U.S. beef
- Population/high urbanization rates
- High disposable income
- Do people go out to eat?
- Affinity for U.S. brands

But failing to find data on "Do people go out to eat?" or "Affinity for U.S. brands," he largely dismissed these. One measure for "Affinity for U.S. brands" might be to see how other beef-serving restaurants are doing in that country. Outback Steakhouse, for example, has this on their Web site (http://www.outbacksteakhouse.com/ourlocations/international.asp) and clicking on a specific country will reveal all of its Outback restaurants.

Good market selection followed by the wrong mode of entry is a recipe for disaster. Likewise, poor market selection can rarely, if ever, be fixed by a good mode of entry strategy. The variables that must be considered if moving from franchising to either a joint venture or company-owned stores are largely legal issues. Managers can list all the potential modes of entry, which can be placed in three general categories, as seen in Figure 10.2. It can be useful to note that something which seems counterintuitive at first—that risk increases as control increases—is in fact the case. The more a company invests, the greater the control, but the greater the capital is at risk, too.

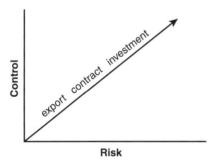

Figure 10.2 Modes of entry categories available for Ruth's Chris

Some reasons for choosing a particular country can include:

• Home country similarities
• Existing countries
• Ease of entry
• Inquiries from country

- Opportunity cost of studies
- Management preferences

Management preference is a classic nonquantitative issue. One preference might be to not even pursue international business, an issue hinted at in this case. Thus, a quick review of the advantages of internationalization might be useful, including income diversity, currency diversity, new sourcing channels, and building a global brand to increase valuation.

In general, a SWOT analysis of Ruth's Chris might prove instructive. Some of the SWOT issues believed to be important are:

Strengths

- Strong U.S. brand
- Profitable company
- Profitable domestic and international franchisees
- Strong balance sheet following 2005 IPO
- Ten international restaurants on two continents

Weaknesses

- Very limited international brand
- Limited international experience
- Not focused on international expansion
- Single mode of entry experience
- Only fine dining product
- No global partners

Opportunities

- Declining chicken consumption (bird flu)
- High beef consumption
- Good reputation for American beef and fine dining
- Tourist familiarization with Ruth's Chris

- Regionalization of tastes
- Success of American franchises

Threats

- Anti-U.S. sentiment
- Global recession
- Failure to conclude successful free-trade agreements
- Decline of Atkins diet formula or other health concerns
- Mad cow and other beef-related diseases

Hannah had many years of experience in the restaurant franchising business and thus had both personal preferences and good instincts about where Ruth's Chris should be looking for new markets. But prior to his arrival, the company had largely allowed franchisees to choose Ruth's Chris, rather than using a more proactive approach.

A quantitative approach offered Hannah a chance to validate his instincts. He asked a team of local MBA students to work down the beef-eaters index in Table 6.5 (in Chapter 6). He eliminated those countries that did not allow the importation of U.S. beef (like the European Union [EU]) and discounted those with low per capita GDPs or small populations. For the initial cut, the team chose not to focus on whether or not people in those countries ate out (they did not have a source of reliable data). Also, they did not want to eliminate those countries without an affinity for U.S. brands, in part because companies like Starbucks and McDonald's had been successful in places with governments hostile to the United States. The brands had an impact on the people that their governments could not (or chose not to) counter politically or culturally.

Finally, because Hannah wanted geographic diversity in the target list, the best prospects on three different continents were selected, based on weighing the beef-eaters index more heavily than the other two factors. An initial list of best prospects included the following countries by region:

Asia	Latin America	Europe
Singapore	Chile	Switzerland
Japan	Brazil	
South Korea	Argentina	
UAE (Dubai)	Costa Rica	
China		
Israel		

Hannah reconstituted this list based on his instincts, existing inquiries from would-be franchisees, and his perception of their receptivity to a U.S fine dining restaurant.

Asia	Latin America	Europe
Japan	Honduras	Switzerland
UAE (Dubai)	Costa Rica	
Singapore	Brazil	
South Korea	Chile	
China	Argentina	

For Asia, the existing franchisee, who had been so successful in Taiwan, had contacts in Japan and wanted to pursue that market, first in Tokyo. The company had already received inquiries about Dubai. And Singapore, South Korea (Seoul), and China (Shanghai) were all solid prospects with highly successful existing restaurant franchises. South Korea, for example, had more Outback Steakhouses than any other country in the world other than the United States.

For South America, Hannah had identified and met with a would-be franchisee who wanted to develop much of Central America. Brazil and Chile had many successful existing restaurant franchises. And Argentina had one of the highest beef consumption rates on the continent, but a strong preference for the taste of its own very robust local beef production.

For Europe, Switzerland offered a chance to sneak behind EU enemy lines and plant a flag on the continent. The United Kingdom would certainly be a highly desirable market if U.S. beef could be imported.

Chapters 7 and 8: The Athlete's Foot Master Franchisee in China

Franchising in China is a relatively new and growing phenomenon that has gained momentum since the 1990s. Among the franchising pioneers in China are large and well-known food and beverage brands, such as KFC and McDonald's. Less well known, but equally important, are the nonfood retailing and service industries, which also made inroads in China using franchising. One such example is the case of The Athlete's Foot, Inc. This American company has been a major competitor in the athletic shoes and sportswear sectors globally. It made an early entry into China using master international franchising and, consequently, ran into problems that are often encountered when companies expand internationally using franchising.

Part A of the case in Chapter 7 describes franchising in China, The Athlete's Foot, Inc., and the experiences of the Chinese master franchisee—Rick Wang. Despite the initial success of this franchise system in China, Wang quickly ran into financial and operational problems. Part B in Chapter 8 illustrates what Wang did to rescue the company from its problems.

Entrepreneurs choose franchising as the approach to initiate their business when they have an adequate amount of funding but less-than-optimal business experience. The following key aspects should be carefully considered while preparing to become a master franchisee:

Opportunity research and predictions of:

- Market demand
- Market size

- Market structure and competition
- Margin analysis

Find an appropriate partner with whom to build a franchise relationship, ideally one who has:

- Experience and a reputation in franchising (market presence, market share, number of company owned outlets)
- Outlet performance experience
- Knowledge of the business format (training, operations systems, field support)
- An understanding of the terms of the licensing agreement
- A market-development plan
- An understanding of the intricacies of franchise fees and royalties
- Knowledge of available resources, avenues of supply, and so forth, specific to the target environment

Create a detailed plan for business operations, including:

- Site selection
- Outlet construction
- Employee training
- Inventory and operations management
- Advertising and market promotion
- Supply chain

Using the above lists as an approach to analyzing The Athlete's Foot case, we can summarize the key points as follows.

Market Opportunity

The targeted (ideal) customer base is fashion-conscious 20- to 35-year-olds. This customer group expands as brand loyalty is inculcated in the target culture. The purchasing power of this demographic, especially in big cities in the more-urbanized and developed coastal areas, makes this a highly desirable group for retailers of Western goods. The size of this market group in the booming Chinese economy adds to its allure. Competition in the early stages of The Athlete's Foot's establishment in China was weak, but it increased sharply as more players joined the game. Profit margins are high as costs (especially for labor and production) are relatively low.

Ultimately, these market factors and the target demographic combined to create a promising initial opportunity for The Athlete's Foot franchise, though increased competition would heighten the problems associated with an "easy" sense of how business would proceed.

Franchise Relationship

The Athlete's Foot, Inc., as an international franchisor with a 30-year history, has extensive international franchise experience. Its global market presence, good outlet performance, service innovation, and standardized operations format all provide evidence of its competence. To build a franchise relationship, The Athlete's Foot, Inc., offered Wang and his colleague valuable operational training, negotiated a franchisor-friendly license with Wang, and granted Wang the exclusive franchise license in China's mainland market. Thanks to the consensus of franchisor and franchisee, the process of building the franchise relationship was smooth, appropriately formal, yet quick. Both parties operated well together, creating a collaborative enterprise with a promising future. Cooperation enabled initial success.

However, The Athlete's Foot, Inc., entered the Chinese market with some glaring levels of ignorance and no "presence" upon which to immediately draw. It had little knowledge of the intricacies of the Chinese market and slight experience in dealing with local vendors. When the franchisee (Wang) began to have trouble, the franchisor could do little to assist him. The franchisor, in fact, did not effectively participate in the development of the Chinese market, but left most of the control in the hands of the franchisee. Any partnership can disintegrate when partners are not equal to the tasks associated with the business.

Business Operations

Adequate attention was paid to retail site selection, outlet construction, employee training, inventory, and operations management. The initial outlet was located in an appropriate venue. It was attracting customers through its superior products, innovative store environment, and customer-oriented service.

Advertising and promotion, however, were not effective enough. Retail brand marketing neither reached target customers nor built a strong brand image. The sports retailing brand ("The Athlete's Foot") failed to root in the minds of target customers. Clients were loyal to retailing products not to the retailing venue.

Supply-chain management was especially weak. Lack of leverage on major suppliers led directly to the company's major crisis.

To explain the problems in Wang's company, managers can use the "SWOT" method to give an overview of the company.

Internal Strengths

- High-quality products
- Superior retailing facility
- Trained staff
- Customer-oriented service
- International brand image
- Superior technological skill in inventory
- Innovative operations model (franchise)
- First-mover advantage in an emerging market

Internal Weaknesses

- Lack of solid experience and market knowledge of retailing sector
- Lack of strong relationships with key suppliers
- Lack of core competence and effective long-term strategy
- Inadequate financial support for the potential size of market (self-financed)
- Comparatively weak franchisor
  - Failure to provide adequate support to franchisee
  - Inadequate relationships with key vendors
  - Premature launch into Chinese market

External Opportunities

- Large market base
- Rapid and steady increase in demand
- Regulatory environment improved

External Threats

- Market share was squeezed by more competitors
- Reluctant cooperation of suppliers
- Rental cost rose

Initially, Rick Wang ran his company quite well in a competition-free market where there was abundant product demand and less competition in the target market. He also enjoyed superior management training and a useful operations' model, and learned from his internationally experienced footwear retailing franchisor. During a period of rapid growth, however, the company was more focused on cultivating the market rather than on evaluating weaknesses and identifying inherited problems. Risks were hidden as the company enjoyed its initial successes.

As the external environment changed to a comparatively mature market (with abundant and rapidly growing demands and intense competition), the negative effects of the company's weaknesses became more apparent, leading to a crisis. The impending crisis was made more acute because the company had not established a solid base before launching an aggressive growth strategy. In this case, the more outlets the company had, the larger the damage would be when the market matured.

When considering suggestions to rescue the company from its crisis, students may turn to points of internal weakness and external threats, and then work out plans to avoid these hidden risks and create responses to threats. Case B describes what Rick Wang actually did to save his company. Instructors may use it as a supplement for Case A and to let students discover Wang's actions after they formulate their own, perhaps after class discussion.

Rick did the following:

- Kept to an economy of scale: retreated from department store and moved to street-front outlet
  - High cost (high rental fee), low profit (low popularity)
- Trial of alternative retailing approach: opened online store for selling footwear
  - Unaccepted by most customers as it conflicted with traditional shopping customs
  - Rejected by brand suppliers as it went against their policies
- Sought help from franchisor
  - Ineffective support from franchisor
- Exited from franchise system
  - Transformed into "single-brand" retailer and regained acceptable sales volume and concomitant profits

From Wang's actions (and their consequences), we can conclude that his best approach to long-term survival was, in fact, to exit the franchise system. The failure of Wang's other actions can be explained by an inadequate diagnosis (by the franchisor) of the rooted problem.

The dynamics of the franchisee-franchisor relationship are influenced by four issues: wealth creation, communications, the brand, and exit costs:

- **Wealth creation**—A view by each player about how the franchise system will help them become wealthy, or at least provide a market return on investment.

- **Communications**—Franchising, as a long-term contractual relationship, has many challenges because both people and markets change. A relationship based on both formal and informal methods of communication is at the core of a relationship flexible enough to last over time.

- **Brand**—Both franchisor and franchisee need to collectively value the brand and maintain and build it; only then will the relationship succeed—and yield success.

- **Exit costs**—The franchisee needs to evaluate the long-term value of the relationship versus the cost(s) of exiting the relationship.

Following from the four aspects listed above, an analysis of Wang's transformation can be made. The franchise system brought Wang's company an early success in wealth creation; however, profits sharply declined as market conditions changed. Wang had little support from the franchisor during the company's crisis—a situation that was exacerbated because the brand was not yet solidly established in the Chinese market. Wang believed his exit costs were acceptable when compared with the losses inherent in keeping the franchise afloat and the franchise relationship intact. Additionally, the ambiguities of the legal environment at the time contributed to regulatory inconsistency.

Like brand establishment, this was a crucial problem that should have been both the primary responsibility of the franchisor and effectively communicated to the franchisee.

Chapter 9: Organic Farming Microfranchising in Indonesia

"Social entrepreneurs act as society's change agents, seizing opportunities others miss and improving systems, inventing new approaches, and creating solutions to change society for the better. Rather than leaving societal needs to the government and business sectors, they find what is not working and solve the problem by changing the system, spreading the solution, and persuading entire societies to take new leaps."[11] Oded Carmi was one such entrepreneur striving for a "green Bali." He started *Sari Organik* as a model farm intended to grow organically with market demand and benefit the local community while serving as an educational center for small-scale farmers in the region. Thirteen years down the line, the idea was not as well embraced as he had hoped.

The case provides information on social entrepreneurship, gives a background on Carmi, the environment in Ubud, Bali, and Indonesia at large, and discusses some of the challenges the entrepreneur was facing as the founder and owner of the *Sari Organik* farm and the restaurant *Warung Bodag Maliah* (overflowing basket). His main challenge was to replicate and sustain his organic rice-farming model across Bali and eventually other parts of Indonesia. His initial thoughts involved some options:

- To utilize the established village system and its leadership (religious and civil) to reintroduce traditional rice-farming culture in Ubud, Bali, and eventually Indonesia

- To introduce a new model such as microfranchising through which he (the microfranchisor) would recruit a number of local farmers (microfranchisees) and provide them with the resources to grow rice organically

- To go into a joint venture with the few existing organic rice farmers in the region

- To expand his business as a sole proprietor, that is, to buy more land and increase organic rice production—this was his least favorite option because it would go against his mission of involving the community

The case may be a good starting point for discussion on the impact of modernization on a traditional society and the role of business in society. Carmi, a native of Israel, tried to revive traditional farming techniques that were more sustainable and healthy. He realized he had to come up with a strategy soon, and was open to other viable options for replication and sustenance.

Doing business in Bali, and Indonesia generally—a largely collectivist society that recognizes and values its village system as an administrative structure and respects its leadership—requires, most importantly, the support of the village leaders (religious and civil). It would be advantageous to have these leaders act as ambassadors for *Sari Organik's* organic rice-farming model, using the respect they command through their power and influence to convince the community that this business model is both respectable and sustainable and would improve not only the health of the community, but also their economy.

The Indonesian business environment can be summarized as follows using the PEST framework:

Political

- Government involved in legal and economic reforms
- Bureaucracy ranks high and lack of transparency is a big issue

- Ranked 122nd on ease of doing business, 161st on starting a business, 113th on getting credit, 142nd on closing a business
- Requires patience and an understanding of influences affecting business culture and legal and regulatory environments
- Gained independence from the Netherlands in 1949, but only held its 1st free parliamentary election in 1999, ending a repressive rule
- The third-largest democracy after India and the United States
- World's largest archipelagic state (three times the size of Texas)
- Ranks 10th to 25th percentile on political stability (WGI 2008)
- Ranks 25th to 50th percentile on voice and accountability, government effectiveness, regulatory quality, rule of law, and control of corruption (WGI 2008)

Economical

- Labor consists of agriculture, 42%; industry, 18%; services, 39% (2006)
- Relies mainly on domestic consumption as the driver of economic growth—considered an emerging market
- Increasing GDP; ranked 16th in the world with PPP at $969 billion, 33rd with real growth rate at 4.5%, and 155th with per capita PPP at $4,000 (2009)
- GDP composition by sector—agriculture, 15%; industry, 47%; services, 37% (2009)
- Ranks 78th with an unemployment rate of 7% (2009), and 17% of population under poverty level (2006)
- Has a high level of inequality of power and wealth
- Ranks 142nd with an inflation rate of 4.8% (2009)
- Central bank discount rate of 10% and commercial bank prime lending rate of 13% (2008)
- Indonesian rupiahs (IDR) per U.S. dollar = 10,399.2 (2009)

Social-Cultural

- Challenges: Poverty, unemployment, inadequate infrastructure, underdeveloped education, corruption, human rights violations, complex regulatory environment, separatist movement, and unequal resource distribution

- Home to the world's largest Muslim population (approximately 86%, 2010); Protestants, 5%; Catholics, 3%; Hindus, 1%; others, 3%

- Ranks high on power distance at 78 (United States, 40), 48 on uncertainty avoidance (United States, 46), 14 on individualism—a collectivist society (United States, 91), and 46 on masculinity (United States, 62)

- 4th most populous country in the world after China, India, and the United States (approximately 242 million, 2010)

- Age structure: 0–14, 27%; 15–64, 66%; 65 and over, 6% (2009)

- Ranks 110th with a population growth rate of 1% (2010)

- 52% urban population; 3.3% annual growth (2008)

Technological

- 45,000 square kilometers of land irrigated; only 11% arable land (2003)

- Need for sustainable development (going green)—manage natural resources; poverty reduction; and human development

- Weather—tropical; hot, humid; more moderate in highlands

- Poor infrastructure and underdeveloped education

- Environmental challenges: deforestation; water pollution from industrial wastes, sewage; air pollution in urban areas; smoke and haze from forest fires

- Ranks 10th in the world for main line telephone use at 30 million, and 6th for cellular use at 140 million (2006)

- Ranks 42nd in the world for Internet hosts with 865,000 (2009)

- Access to airports (10th in the world), heliports, pipelines, railways (25th), roadways (13th), waterways (5th) (2008)

- Terrain—mostly coastal lowlands; some interior mountains

The case suggests that there is a growing movement of people who would like to readopt traditional rice-farming practices and also indicates that a cultural argument for change could work in this region. Mr. Carmi expresses his concerns regarding the current condition of the Subak system, but he is confident that the competitive atmosphere can be turned around to its original cooperative nature.

It sounds like the community needs to be reminded of the Tri Hita Karana philosophy, and this should then be tied in with the benefits of growing rice organically. Because the government is now supportive of this farming model, and a change in the farmers' perspectives seems to be taking place already, the model just needs to be implemented at the village level, with the help of the village leaders and buy-in from the community so that they all readopt it.

It seems fitting for Mr. Carmi to consider adopting a microfranchising model because it would act as an economic development tool that would help him introduce his organic rice-farming model as a scaled-down business concept to the local farmers and would necessitate the replication and sustenance of this venture. The idea of adopting a microfranchising model seems to promote Mr. Carmi's mission for *Sari Organik* and would involve community effort as compared with going it alone.

A joint venture with other organic rice farmers, for example, The Big Tree Farm and Pegasus Farm, sounds like a viable option, although the case does not provide evidence indicating that the other farmers would be willing to consider this option.

Mr. Carmi's microfranchisees would generally be fledgling microentrepreneurs; they would need his support, as well as training both in organic farming and business operation and management. The start-up costs of microfranchises are usually minimal, but the farmers would still need his help in securing microcredit through microfinancing institutions in order to purchase the necessary equipment and farm inputs, and cover operating expenses. Being novices at running a business and lacking access to infrastructure, the microfranchisees would also need advertising and sales support.

Mr. Carmi can maintain control by avoiding a "turnkey" strategy. He should help the farmers set up their businesses, provide them with the necessary support, and, like a franchisor, outline the desired quality standards and operating procedures, establish a monitoring and reporting system in order to hold microfranchisees accountable, use both qualitative and quantitative data to predict and preclude potential challenges, and also diagnose and resolve operating issues.

Mr. Carmi first needs to ascertain that his microfranchise is replicable for other individuals/areas and then needs to establish relationships with potential microfinance institutions (because microfranchisees need financing to start their enterprises). He then needs to identify potential microfranchisees, train them, and assist them in implementing the business. Once the enterprises are up and running, he needs to provide day-to-day support as outlined above.

Mr. Carmi can combat his competition by focusing on the offerings he provides through *Sari Organik* that the competitors do not (differentiation). He should define and target a specific market niche, rather than trying to be a "jack-of-all-trades," and excel at serving that niche. Because his competitors may provide different offerings, he could work with them, supply them with things they need, and purchase some of their offerings, thus building a healthy relationship with them. He should make every reasonable effort to learn from established organic farmers and microfranchises using the same model, find ways to capture and sustain local business before expanding to other regions, and also be visible and active locally through community groups, activities, and initiatives.

Summary

We hope that this book is a good overview of the franchising industry as it is going internationally, to emerging markets, and to culturally and physically distant countries. The diversity of countries and industries will prove to be a guiding force for those who want to learn about the key success factors of franchising globally. Across countries and industries, analyses can help identify both commonalities and differences among these success factors.

Endnotes

1. "Taking Over," *The Economist*, May 15, 1999, 5.

2. M&S (Marks & Spencer) Press Releases (1999): www.marks-and-spencer.co.uk/corporate/press-releases/19990518.002.html (accessed May, 27, 1999).

3. Dow Jones Industrial, "Executive Report Marks & Spencer PLC," http://mrstg1s.djnr.com/cgi-bin/DJIntera..._binding=&get_name=null&searchText=U.MAR (accessed May 26, 1999).

4. "Angst in Their Pants," *Financial Times Weekend FT* 37 (June 1999): 7–10.

5. M&S (Marks & Spencer) Press Releases (1999): www.marks-and-spencer.co.uk/corporate/press-releases/19990518.002.html (accessed May 27, 1999).

6. Ibid.

7. Alexandra Jardin, "St. Michael's Evangelist," *Marketing*, April 22, 1999, 25–28.

8. M&S (Marks & Spencer) Press Releases (1999): www.marks-and-spencer.co.uk/corporate/press-releases/19990518.002.html (accessed May 27, 1999).

9. Ibid.

10. At the time of writing, the British pound/dollar exchange is 0.6283, July 11, 2011.

11. "What Is a Social Entrepreneur?" www.ashoka.org/social_ entrepreneur (accessed May 28, 2011).

Index